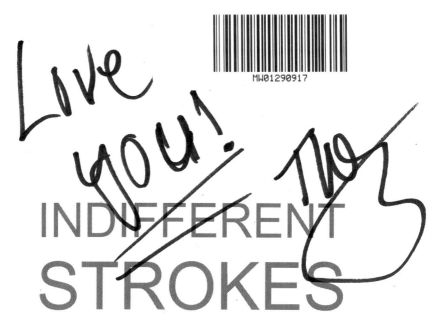

INDIFFERENT STROKES

EMBRACING LIFE'S ADVERSITIES

Love you!

Be a Miracle!

TERRANCE MINNOY

MW01290917

ISBN-13: 978-1987629484
ISBN-10:1987629485

DEDICATION

First, I dedicate this book to the memory of my loving mother, Dorothy L. Coleman, who nurtured the spirit of resilience and drive in my life. Thank you for making sure I was introduced to Jesus Christ.

I also dedicate this book to my children, Taylor, Ryan, and Devin. I consider each of you my WHY. Devin, I consider you one of my heroes. I feel that God decided to use you to save my life. He did that for a reason. Consider it another gift. Use it.

Lastly, I dedicate this book to every person that visited me in the hospital, sent words of sympathy and encouragement, supported and prayed for me. Some of you even prayed with me. Thank you to each person that has pushed this book out of me and did not allow me to sit on my gifts, passion, and story.

CONTENTS

FOREWORD

"The Universe Talks To You" is one of the many chapters inside of **INDIFFERENT STROKES - EMBRACING LIFE'S ADVERSITIES.** When I read this chapter I said to myself, "Wow! This is the most realist passage I've read in a long time." During the course of your lifespan, you will be put up against this thing called life and in this chapter, Terrance talks about paying attention to the Universe so you're able to hear it when it speaks to you. So what does this mean? Think about this. As you're moving forward in life, roadblocks or situations will come at you from many directions. Divorces, Job loss, Health issues, Family separation, Loss wages, etc. While going through these situations you will surely question why these things are happening to you. That's reality. But then, what tends to happen? Once you have climbed up out of that setback, and you're finally seeing the light, and things are going better than your previous situation, *THAT* is when you get that Oprah "aha" moment. *THAT* is when you begin to remember why things had happen. *THAT* is paying attention to the Universe. But what could've happened if you paid a little more attention to the universe *BEFORE* the situation arise? You think the outcome would've been different? Maybe. This is what Terrance talks about in this chapter. Terrance makes it very clear on why it is important to pay attention to the Universe when it's talking to you.

Terrance "Miracle" Minnoy and I met because we chose to pay attention to the Universe. The plans to have Terrance's book in his hand in order to give you the tips and tools on how to survive the "strokes" in your life, was birthed prior to meeting me (a Book Coach), and prior to having his strokes.

Paying attention to the Universe is key and I'm going to give you a quick glimpse on how this Universe road map works as I sum it up from his book:

1. December 2014, Terrance purchased a new unwanted Disability Policy plan
2. January 2015, he noted "Motivational Speaker" and "Author" on his vision board

3. Top of the year 2015, his son Devin, moved into his house earlier than expected

4. February 2015, he suffered three strokes in 24 hours

5. His son, Devin (who moved in with him) called 911 and saved his life

6. His income dropped down to 75% (less $1000 earnings) and ironically, that unwanted policy was for $1000

7. He relearned how to walk & documented the journey

8. He was interviewed regarding his story by the same hospital who nursed him back to health

9. He continued to tell his story

10. One year after the strokes he post a video of his survival which went viral

11. The video was posted on many timelines, including mine which started our introduction

12. I'm a Book Coach

13. Terrance wrote "**INDIFFERENT STROKES**"

Did you see how that journey mapped out? The Universe will talk to you if you pay attention. Terrance had an original thought of becoming an author, but only God knew what he was up against in order to make that happen. Unfortunately, Terrance had to suffer 3 strokes in 24 hours in order to give you the product God has crafted for you. Could Terrance have moped around after his strokes waiting for people to care for him? Yes, he could have.

However, Terrance had already put his success in the atmosphere which changed his course in life.

Many people will mope around after a tragedy or a situation that arise in their life but **INDIFFERENT STROKES** is here to show you that you cannot absolutely live there. You're greater than that and if you follow these certain tools that is written in this book, you will be on your way to living a better life.

Now, embrace yourself. This ride you are about to embark on in reading **INDIFFERENT STROKES** will be a bit bumpy. Be prepared to get the unapologetically, raw, and transparent Terrance Minnoy. **INDIFFERENT STROKES** is compelling, captivating, and motivating at the same time. Terrance has had a lot of setbacks in life so it was important to highlight those while being relatable and transparent for his readers. In working with Terrance, he was specific on what he wanted his readers to grab from his book. His goal was to reach the individuals who felt stuck in life. The ones who felt they couldn't bounce back from certain situations. The ones who felt they couldn't see beyond what was in front of them. These are the readers Terrance prayed that he would reach. His focus was on the readers who needed that extra nudge to help get them to that next level of success in life. He executed this in every way. Not only are these tools helpful for the readers, Terrance applies these same tools within his own life.

INDIFFERENT STROKES has motivated me in every way and I'm here to tell you to get your highlighters, notepads, and ink pens ready because the notes you are about to take will be life changing! Take in this journey... be INDIFFERENT.

-

Chantay E. Brown

Author/ Motivational Speaker/ Book Coach

WHY THIS BOOK?

Let's set the tone for this read right up front. This will not be a difficult read. I didn't write this book in an attempt to advance my literary skills. I didn't write this book to brand myself. I'm a capitalist through-and-through but I didn't write this book with dreams of adding to my cache or my financial portfolio. So why did I write this book? Well that's a reasonable question and I'll answer it in a few minutes. But first, let me ask you a couple questions. These questions may involve reader participation so be a good sport and play along.

As a youth I used to play this game with my friends or family. I don't know the name of it anymore. Maybe you do. It's a simple game. Let's just call it, the "touch" game. The idea was for you to stand still silently and motionless with your eyes open. The other participant would stand directly in front of you at arm's length.

They would extend one of their arms with their index finger pointing at you. They would place that index finger directly, I mean within inches, of your nose. They couldn't touch your nose or they'd be disqualified. Each of you would get a turn to be the "index man" and the other, the "nose man". Are you still with me? Great if you are. If you're a little confused, keep reading anyway.

The goal of the game is whoever could stand having the index finger placed in front of their nose without moving away or rubbing their nose, wins! It's that simple. And if you like, you can play the game right now. If there is no one with you right now that's ok, you can actually play the game alone as well. Simply place your index finger directly in front of your nose without touching it. Now, when you're playing the game, here's what's going to happen whether you play the game with someone else or by yourself.

As the finger lingers slightly in front of your nose without it touching you, you will strangely start feeling a tingle at the tip and bridge of your nose. This feeling becomes more intense the longer the finger is near your nose; so intense that eventually you'll have to move away from the finger and rub your nose because it feels like you're being touched. It's like an itch that you have to scratch.

Life is just like that index finger. In order for you to do anything else in life, you must first address the itch by scratching it which in turn, subsides the irritating feeling in your face. I'm sure you've dealt with this feeling before when you've had an intense itch in the middle of your back and you couldn't reach it with your hands. So what did you do before you did anything else? You either ask someone to scratch your back, or you found an object long enough that you could use to reach the itch. Lastly, you'd turn around, place your back on the corner of a wall and commence to doing squats in order to align that itch with the surface of the wall to give you a much needed scratch of relief. Ok, I'm done with that analogy. I assume you get the point by now.

"So Terrance, why did you write this book?" I wrote this book because for the past 5 years there has been a finger in front of my nose giving me these occasional intense urges to scratch my nose or wipe away that "feeling". I had to react and finally address this ginormous urge in my gut and heart to publically share my thoughts through writing. This urge intensifies ten-fold when I think about the millions of people that I'm supposed to serve. This is one of my vehicles to do so. This itch has to be scratched but for more reasons than relieving an internal itch to touch others. I believe that my life was specifically planned out and navigated so that I'd experience every possible human emotion and circumstance. These experiences were tattered with happiness, feelings of ecstasy, elation, wonderful adrenaline rushes, hope, and love. They were also mixed with intense feelings of failure, guilt, worthlessness, uncertainty, fear, condemnation, anger, and sorrow. Maybe you know exactly what I'm talking about. As they say, "Am I on your street?"

So with all of that said, the answer to the question of why I wrote this book is a resounding, "I had to!" The scratching of this itch had to be done in order for me to feel completely comfortable moving on as a contributor in the field of personal development, motivational speaking, and coach. I thunderously and victoriously have overcame monumental moments of cruel treatment, self inflicted pain, embarrassments, shame, failure, loss, and a life changing near-death experience. Needless to say, the index finger has been one centimeter from the tip of my nose for quite some time now. The feeling is unbearable! This book is the corner of the wall that I need to scratch that unreachable irritating itch.

I receive favor in such an abundant amount. The Creator has been so merciful throughout my life. Even when the wiles of this world, the evil, and unpleasant touch me in some way, I'm left wounded but never defeated. This knowledge further intensifies the feeling I have inside to react, move on, and share my story of resilience and strategies to master setbacks. Yes, you can master your setbacks! You don't have to just be a punching bag...the penetrable sparring partner for life's adversities. As a matter of fact, you can give adversity a strong embrace and make failure your friend by mastering the control of your internal thermometer, and developing a lifestyle of self confrontation and self improvement.

In closing, this book is full of analogies that'll make you analyze all of your actions and reactions when it comes to adversities in your life. By the end, my hope is that your belief is heightened with the knowledge that tough moments that arrive in our lives can be embraced as gifts. There are a few "how to's" in this book but the main tools that I use are stories, philosophies, and principles that'll help shape your thinking which in turn attracts the success you're searching for, the healing that you need, and the positive universal energy that elevates every area of our lives.

"OK life! You've had your finger in my face for a long time. I'm tired of this feeling. I'm feverishly and happily scratching it. It's on!"   *- Terrance*

THESE AIN'T JOKES

"These ain't jokes", is what Nathaniel Stroman says consistently throughout his comedy routines. Usually immediately after his punch-lines, he uses this now infamous quote to make the point that he has literally lived the situations he jokes about. This is usually followed by raucous laughter from the audience.

His stage name is Earthquake. Maybe you've heard of him before? I like his humor but I more so like his usage of the statement, "These ain't jokes". Now, I know it's not grammatically correct but I like it. It resonates with me. It speaks to one of my favorite words, authenticity. I find that I'm attracted to authentic things. Real things. Real stories. Real people.

My favorite genre of music is hip-hop. Hip-Hop music is known to sample old music to create a new sound. I don't mind the new-age sound of hip-hop at times but soon I find myself googling the older sampled record, within the record. I want to know all about it. Who made it? How old is it? Who produced it? etc. I do the same thing when I'm watching an interesting movie, especially when it's a remake. I want to know more about the original. I want to know more about its authenticity. How true is it to the original story? I recently did this with the movie Scarface starring Al Pacino. Did you know that it's a remake of the original film of the same name? It was released in 1932 and it starred Paul Muni. I'm fascinated with authenticity. I'm fascinated with real stories and real feelings.

I'm going to share some real stories and real feelings in this book. With authenticity I'll share stories, strategies, and philosophies that will move you to take action in your life. You will be encouraged to pursue your dreams and goals while still enjoying the purposeful work you are currently doing. Many circumstances and situations I've personally faced will only allow me to write from the most authentic place of my soul. Therefore, my grammar won't be perfect nor will my usage of proper punctuation always be correct. I hope you can manage to receive my message regardless. What you'll eventually attest to is that my passion and conviction is perfect! I believe every word, strategy, concept, and recommendation in this book is perfect. It's perfect because it's authentic. Earthquake says, "These ain't jokes". I say, "These ain't made up stories". I don't want to motivate and inspire you solely based on just stories I've heard throughout my life or massive research that I've done. I'm going to let my own personal story do the "heavy lifting". I think you'll get more out of this book if I reach into the depths of my soul and memory to give you something. I want to give you something that'll increase your desire to wholeheartedly, and full-speed ahead pursue the best version of yourself. I believe that listening to authentic words of inspiration is a "flame thrower" in a knife fight. Yes, I said a knife fight. There is an internal fight happening within your mind and soul. It's a constant and continuous fight. You hear the rumblings of the fisticuffs daily telling you that you can't, you're too tired, that's too hard, you're not special, you don't have the talent, you're too old, it's too cold outside, you failed before, don't try again, lower your expectations, you're not the right nationality, being average is ok... Should I continue? You see, I'm so authentic I even know what the voices are saying inside your head. Those thoughts and voices are strong and piercing like a knife. They slowly cut away any semblance of courage or ingenuity. For most, this cutting process usually starts in adolescence and continues throughout your productive years. Eventually the knife reaches the heart and begins to poke holes and then you die. Unfortunately for most though, this death happens before your actual physical manifestation of death. As Benjamin Franklin said, "Some people die at 25 and aren't buried until 75."

On the other hand, some people don't have a story that's as dismal as what I just described. They come to the fight with flame throwers. Authentic words of inspiration and motivation have equipped them with the tools that make the fight almost unfair. Most of the time they incinerate most of those voices. They don't give them a chance to reach the depths of the soul or to pierce at the heart. This is what authentic coaching can and will do for you. This book will give you just that. Read on.

INDIFFERENCE

Why Indifference?

You're likely scratching your head right now (literally or figuratively) after reading the title to this book. I can hear it now, "Indifferent? As in the popular 80's sitcom, Diff'rent Strokes? You're likely saying, "What you talkin 'bout Willis?" No, I mean, "What you talkin' 'bout Terrance?" Well, I'll tell you exactly what I'm talking about.

Later in this book I will boldly state that everyone has a "stroke" in their lives. As a matter of fact, most people have multiple strokes in their lives. These strokes have either crippled them or possibly set their lives on an upward trajectory. I can attest to the latter.

In the literal sense, a stroke is a "brain attack". The blood flow to the brain has been drastically interrupted and usually a blood clot is the cause. This eventually causes brains cells to die and significantly affects the nervous system's ability to function properly. This can happen in our lives as well. Here are the areas of our lives that can suffer a stroke…an attack.

Finances

Relationships

Social life

Mental

Physical

Spiritual

Career

Business

Vocabulary.com states: *(noun) "Indifference is the trait of lacking interest or enthusiasm in things. When you feel indifference for something, you neither, like it nor dislike it.*" It goes on to say that indifference is the *"trait of remaining calm and seeming not to care; a casual lack of concern."* You see, when a stroke happens in our lives we must respond to it and be careful not to overly react to it. As they say, it's better to have a positive response to medication rather than to have a reaction to medication. When dealing with these strokes in our lives it's all about how we respond to them. We should do the best that we can to NOT have too much of a reaction to them. So, in this book when I use the words indifference or indifferent, I'm referring only to our responses to the attacks in various areas of our lives. We should be indifferent when we are taking on each step in our process to recover or effort to bounce back.

Indifference can be a good thing…no, a great thing if it's used correctly in certain moments. Here are three ways indifference can play a very important role in your ability to respond to strokes in your lives.

• REMAINING CALM, POISED, AND CALCULATING AT ADVERSITY'S POINT-

OF-ATTACK. Take in the information. Evaluate your necessary response time. Be still and quiet.

- **DURING THE ATTACK, UNWAVERING CONFIDENCE IN YOUR ABILITY TO NAVIGATE YOUR JOURNEY THROUGH THE STORM.** The Bible says, "This too shall pass". This isn't your first stroke or storm. Remember that and courageously deal with the situation. Hold your head high.

- **LACKING INTEREST IN OUTER AND INTERNAL VOICES OF DOUBT, NEGATIVITY, AND LIMITED THINKING.** Ignore that voice in your head that tends to make the situation worse than it really is. That voice gives birth to doubt. Stay positive and **EXPECT** things to work out for you.

We'll further explore each of these throughout the book. Not only will I discuss them but I will also share my real-life experiences in applying indifference in order to make a tremendous difference in my response and outcome to adverse moments in my life. And in my case, actual strokes too.

IT'S NOT ABOUT YOU

I soon realized that making my experience only about me wasn't going to do me any good. I considered it counterproductive. I was taught early in life by my late mother, Dorothy Coleman, in all situations look for an opportunity to help someone else. As shocking as the events were, I found a way to become more unselfish. The more I gave to considering other people, the better I felt about my situation. Call me crazy but I even felt healing and progress. This helped me maintain my attitude of indifference towards my process of recovery.

Do you want to recover or bounce back? Want your relationship to improve? Want to shine in your career after getting a disappointing job rating? Would you like to see your children do better in school after they had to be held back a grade? How about bouncing back at even a higher level than you've ever been? This can happen! I'm a living witness to it.

Your success isn't just about you, nor is your setbacks. The events may only seem personal but they're not. Someone in a similar situation is better served by knowing your story of resilience or hearing your words of encouragement and inspiration. I'll even take it a step further and say that your resilience can have a rippling effect of which you have no control. It can reverberate across your town. Across your state. Across the county. And even across the world! You may not have any idea. I think this is the best! I know for a fact that I can unknowingly help many more people than I could knowingly. Your story of resilience through indifference may be overheard by someone who then shares the story with someone in need. Someone that you likely don't know. Someone that you'll never meet but you made a difference in their lives.

After 21 days of being hospitalized, I decided to record a "praise report" video and post it on my Facebook timeline. I did this on my last day in rehabilitation center. I was so indifferent to my process of recovery that I wanted to share some tips and spread some encouragement while I was still in the storm. I didn't want to just do a testimonial once I made it out of the storm. We do that most of the time and there's nothing wrong with that. But I wanted to share while I was still in the storm. Post-testimonials are great but I feel that testimonials during the storm are even better for a couple of reasons:

- **IT GIVES THE AUDIENCE A BETTER PICTURE OF WHAT YOU ARE DEALING WITH.** That way, when you overcome, the story is even more encouraging.

- **YOUR ACTIONS TELL THE UNIVERSE THAT YOU ARE CERTAIN THAT YOU WILL BOUNCE BACK.** You are not accepting any negative energy in your life and you demand the universe to show you favor.

Oh yes, you can do that! Shout your request to the Universe!

In this video, I got out of the way. I didn't make the message about me but I decided to give to others. During this message I shared these tips. Whenever you have "life strokes" practice the following:

Have Faith

Show Gratitude

Be Humble

Practice Personal Development

I can't emphasize this point enough. It's not about you at all. You may not have a desire to impact millions like myself and others would like to do, but impacting your immediate family is just as noble and important. Positively impacting your office, your team, your church, and your community is superbly rewarding. If you want to become indifferent to the strokes in your life, embrace this notion, **IT'S NOT ABOUT YOU!**

GIVE IT AWAY

One of the Universal Laws of Success is the "Law of Service" and it says: *Your rewards in life will be in direct proportion to the value of your service to others. The more you work, study, and develop your ability to contribute more to the lives of and well-being of others, the better life you will have in all areas.*

Who doesn't want success? Of course, everyone does. Our appetite for it began when we were an adolescent. No, it began when we were toddlers likely, right? Wrong again, the appetite and tastes of success were birthed in us when we were infants. Oh yes! When we couldn't even walk, talk, or take care of ourselves, we naturally had an appetite for success and we soon learned what the fruits of that success could be. Quite literally, we learned success led us to having some actual fruit! Let me explain.

Through numerous observations over my 47 years on this earth and through personal experience, I've heard this saying;

whenever a baby is crying, "He's hungry", or "She's probably hungry and wants something to eat". Babies learn right away that crying lead to food. Sure there are other reasons babies cry but for this example, let's stick to the need for nourishment. As infants, we learned that a successful cry leads to the satisfaction of fruit in the form of baby food or milk. We soon learned that successfully standing to our feet (even for just a second) lead us to the receiving applause and affection. Success. We learned early on that if we listened to directions or redirection (in most cases) from our parents we learned that it led to receiving praise, recognition, and sometimes more fruit! Success, success, and more SUCCESS. We became addicted to success as infants and eventually it became part of our DNA. Now you may say, "No the baby cries when it is hungry because it innately wants to survive." Yes, exactly! Survival. I dare to say, "If you desire to survive, you desire success." I doubt that there is one person reading this book right now that doesn't want to survive…see tomorrow…have their next meal…get home to their family. You want to survive. Ok, this example may be elementary in some respects but I think you get the point. Our desire for success is rooted in our desire for survival.

Survival is an individual sport that is most manifested in our successful ability to serve someone else. Your level of individual success, in many cases, is in direct proportion to the amount of lives that you positively touch.

In 1991, a group called the Red Hot Chili Peppers came out with a song called, "Give It Away Now". The song became a huge hit for the band and it remains just as popular today. I was in college when the song came out, and I recall hearing that song on a regular basis on road trips with my basketball team. We normally would listen to a popular FM radio station and inevitably they'd play that song. Depending on the length of the road trip, sometimes we'd hear the song a few times. The chorus was very catchy and it would stick in your head for hours after hearing it.

"Give it away, give it away, give it away now
Give it away, give it away, give it away now"

You want success? You want to survive this crazy world at the height of your potential? Give it away! Give it away! You have a multitude of talent (seen and unseen) share it. Give it away! You have a story that others want and need to hear. Tell it. Write the book, blog, or make the speech. Give it away! There is something about your posture and character that makes others feel good about themselves when you're around. That spirit, give it away! Some of you have resources, be it monetary, time, or uplifting words of encouragement and inspiration. Give it away now!

This is the Law of Service at work. Giving it away for the betterment of other people.

EMBRACING THE UNCOMFORT ZONE

There is nothing wrong with being comfortable. I like being comfortable. I do everything that I possibly can to put myself in a comfortable situation. Be it comfort when I'm lying in bed or on the couch watching television. Comfort when it comes to getting a good table at a restaurant. I like being comfortable as well when it comes to my physical fitness. I can surely think of a number of moments that I'm not happy with my physical fitness. Especially after eating a good meal and I look five months pregnant! I'm not comfortable speaking in front of an audience at those times until my stomach deflates. Because of this, I've changed my eating habits for the better.

I like being comfortable when it comes to my finances as well. I go out of my way and make sacrifices because I don't like having credit card debt. I've lived a "check to check" lifestyle before. I didn't like it. Like everyone else, I like the comfort of having a decent balance in my bank accounts. You see, there is nothing wrong with being comfortable. I think being comfortable can put you in a place of progress and success. You can take your life to the next level when you're comfortable. You may not worry as much. You have a routine, but not only do you have a routine, a successful routine. Meaning that you are still able to make life happen and reach for your dreams and goals while in this routine that you have. So the comfort zone isn't always a bad place. I just think that we have to define comfort in a different way. Sometime when you're comfortable it's setting you up so that you can excel in the "uncomfort zone". You have to master your comfort zone in order to excel and see through the murky waters of the non-comfort zone. It's no secret that ultimate success happens when you're outside of your comfort zone. So getting out of your comfort zone is key to your success but to be successful in that zone you have to be on autopilot when it comes to your comfort zone. Know this, your comfort zone can't be a place to be lazy. Comfortable doesn't mean lazy. I'm not speaking about leisure comfort as I spoke about earlier. I'm talking about a comfort zone that helps you get prepared to be successful outside of your comfort zone. Again, it's ok to have a comfort zone as long as it's not just a leisure comfort zone. You want to be comfortable in an environment that constantly stirs you. Not disturbs you...just stirs you. It keeps your emotions and ingenuity going. It keeps you dreaming. Even though you're in your comfort zone you still want to be stirred and wanting to take action on your goals. When you're at peace in that place and making progress in your comfort zone, it makes your journey outside of your comfort zone much more bearable.

We've all heard a variation of the statement, "your success lies outside of your comfort zone". And here's why. While in your comfort zone you are planning, you are bracing yourself and getting ready. Yes, just like a sprinter is getting ready when they get into their starting blocks.

You ever watch world class sprinters run the 100 meter dash? When they are getting in the starting blocks they may wiggle their arms, kick their legs out, stretch their bodies, and take long deep breaths. Prior to that, they were meticulously setting up the starting blocks so that they are comfortable and in their comfort zone before beginning the race. Every person that runs track and uses starting blocks have specific settings for the blocks. I ran track back in my day as a youth. I remember having my specific setting for each foot. I'm right-handed so the right leg tended to be the stronger of my two legs. I usually used that leg to push off to a good start. Then I'd set my left foot at a specific number. I did this to ensure that I was in a comfortable position before starting the race. I wanted to be in my comfort zone. Why? Because I knew that I was about to run into my uncomfort zone. I knew that I was about to stretch myself and put my body under stress for the next 11 seconds. I know what you're likely thinking, "isn't a runner in their comfort zone as well once the race starts?" The answer is yes and no. It's true that a runner is trained to be comfortable during a race. Being comfortable actually aides them in running faster. But the environment of the race is an uncomfortable place once you add the ingredient of competition into it. Now there is strenuous work to be done. Contracting of muscles. Efforts to turn the arms and legs faster. Controlled breathing under strained conditions. Increased heart rate. Sweating. Grunting. There is a lot happening to and around a runner for those few seconds. Not to mention they are now also thinking about keeping their technique and outrunning the rest of the pack. There is quite a bit of agitation being in that space.

Speaking of agitation, let's talk about it for a second. The best example of the power of agitation is our everyday washing machine. Washing machines are able to get our clothes clean because of the agitation it creates. An environment of agitation develops between water, detergent, and clothes. The result of this agitation is clean clothing. The uncomfort zone can play a major role in you coming out of the other side of your mess, victorious and clean.

In life you need your comfort zone. This is your starting block. This is where your adjustments and preparation is happening. You need a place of comfort to get ready for the ultimate race...the race of LIFE! Get ready because life happens. It happens many times when we're shooting for our goals. We want to be better in business, in relationships, in our family, and in many more areas.

We simply want to be better individuals and live up to our full potential. But then this tends to happen. We get into the starting blocks, the gun goes off, and we run directly into our uncomfort zone. We find ourselves agitated. Pushed and pulled in this zone. We get pushed by setbacks and disappointments that happen in our lives. Setbacks like a divorce, a job loss or restructure at the company, the death of a friend or family member, negativity in your family, stuck in traffic on your way to an important meeting, you notice typos on your resume after you have already sent it off, you're not seeing results with your workout regimen, you give in to fast food again and again. I can go on and on. Setback after setback. Disappointment after disappointment. Believe it or not, this is the place that you are most likely to grow. You are most likely to have clarity when it comes to your vision. Speaking for myself, I become incredibly focused, creative, and motivated to make life happen, reach my goals, and attain my dreams whenever a setback happens in my life. When I'm not happy with something in my personal or business life, I tend to use it as fuel. As I laid in a hospital bed for almost a month, I found it to be a great place for growth for me. A more clear vision as to the purpose of my life happened while in the hospital. As I learned to walk again, and dealing with the fact that I almost died due to the three strokes is where my true character was revealed. You are reading this book right now because of that dark situation in my life. I decided to not only share my message but also study how to deliver it more effectively due to this situation I was in. I've simply became a much improved individual thanks to my near-death experience. I've taken my life to higher heights. Author and speaker, Willie Jolley, said that "a setback is just a setup for an incredible comeback". I truly believe that. This was the worse agitation that I've ever had in my uncomfort zone. In life you're going to have multiple uncomfort zones and agitations. Success just isn't outside of your comfort zone. Success is in your uncomfort zones. We should have just one comfort zone, but multiple uncomfort zones. It's just the way life works. Each setback requires us to utilize different tools to overcome and develops us in different ways. We can't use the same tools in every uncomfortable place. I will say that there is a universal "baseline" plan to overcome tough moments. I speak about this plan in my E-Book, "5 Steps to Resilience in Adverse Moments" (located in the back of this book along with the E-Book, "R.E.S.E.T"). Regardless of the setback, in the end we should become better people following tough moments in our lives. Wherever your uncomfort zones may be, you should allow it to develop you in the areas needed.

In order for us to become better in every aspect of "life performance", we must find a place of comfort first! Just as the runner settles in their comfort zone (starting blocks), then the gun goes off and they are chasing their goal of winning the race. They have to run into their uncomfort zone.

This brings me to another point. If you want to be successful, you have to run into your uncomfort zone! You can't tip-toe into your uncomfort zone. You have to go hard! Think about those runners in the 100 meter race. They are running hard. They're making faces. They're grunting and hissing. They are running into that uncomfortable place because they know on the other side of that is victory. Their success, goals, and dreams. Winning!

You may know the story of David and Goliath. It's in the Bible. David was a young and small shepherd boy. Goliath was a nine-foot giant. In 1 Samuel 17:48 (NIV), it states, "As the Philistine (Goliath) moved closer to attack him, David ran quickly toward the battle line to meet him." Without hesitation, David ran towards his uncomfort zone. A place of agitation for him. David slung his rock from his slingshot, hit Goliath in the head and killed him. We have to do that when it comes to pursuing our own goals. We can't tippy-toe with our calling and dreams, we have to be bold and go hard. I'll be honest; I've been guilty of not running towards my obstacles myself at times. There are a few reasons that we do this:

- **Feeling that everything has to be in perfect place**
- **The desire for instant success**
- **Worry about what others may say or think**
- **Listening and believing the voice of doubt in our heads**
- **We don't have tunnel vision - Distracted by others/other things**
- **We do our best to avoid pain**

Let's discuss tunnel vision or the lack of tunnel vision. As a youth I was taught some very important principles about being a sprinter. I was taught to never look back. It slows you down. Don't look to either side. It slows you down and you lose focus. We run this race of life and when we get into our uncomfort zone we can't look back or to the side. Years ago, a mentor of mine, Darnell Self, taught me about "rubbernecking". He told me to avoid it at all cost. Have you ever been behind an accident or stoppage on the the freeway? You're bumper to bumper for a long time so you figure that there has to be something impactful that has happened up ahead. Then once we get to where the incident occured you realized that it was actually an accident that is now being handled on the side of the road. The traffic was backed up and slowed simply because other drivers were "rubbernecking", looking to the side of the road being nosey and paying attention to the traffic accident that is now on the side of the road. This is what happens when we are looking to the side or back when we are running this race called life. We should compete but don't compare. Through our peripheral vision you'll see your competition but don't turn your head to look at them. No need to focus on them. This will slow you down or even make you stop. Have tunnel vision. Go into your uncomfort zone...quickly! Face your challenges head-on with courage.

While in the hospital following my strokes, this is exactly what I did. Once I realized what happened, heard the prognosis from the doctors, and I could see the possibility of never doing some of the things that I loved to do, like walking, running, and jumping, I decided to attack the situation without hesitation...like David. I knew that I had to go for it. I couldn't stand by idly and just take the blows that life was throwing at me. I had to fight back! I had to run into my uncomfort zone because I knew that recovery was on the other side. It's really true that the universe responds to your actions or inaction. It gives you what you want. As much as it likes to hear what you want, it really responds to your actions. It responds to your enthusiastic actions! I smiled lots during my recovery even though my circumstances said that I should not. I went to battle in my uncomfort zone. I can remember shouting this in my head to the uncomfort zone:

"You're not going to hold me back! I'm going to use you. I'm going to use and abuse you. You think you're going to win? No, I'm going to win. Yes, you've had your moment but I'm going to let you know through my words and actions, I'm about to win!"

This is exactly what you should do when you're faced with setbacks and disappointments in the uncomfort zone. Take it a step further. Find a way to smile through it. Your destiny lies on the other side of your comfort zone. You can't avoid the uncomfort zone and the agitation within it. You may not always win the race, but I promise that you'll win YOUR race. You'll become better. You'll learn from the experience. You'll become stronger. You'll bounce back and go to higher heights. Embrace your situation. Run hard. Keep running. Get to the other side. Get to the tape at the finish line. Hopefully you get there first but if not, get there! Finish! That's what life is all about.

TIMING IS EVERYTHING - DEVIN

December 2014

I had just returned from a daddy-daughter trip to New York with my daughter Taylor. We went with Quin and his daughter, Kai. Quin is one of my best friends and we go back to the mid-90's. When I met Quin, I met him at Pepsi-Cola where we worked together at the time. We almost immediately built a big brother-little brother bond and remained that way for quite some time. For some reason, unintentional, our friendship went on hiatus for a long stretch of time. Hey, life happens right? The hiatus was for a few years to be exact. I'd say 3 years plus. Nonetheless, we reconnected as if we never parted...and the bond was even stronger. I believe our bond being stronger 3 years later most likely happened because we both had grew up and experienced life events that inevitably mature you. The most ironic of it all, by the time we got back together we both had young daughters and we were single fathers. Our bond was even more solidified due to that.

It was my first time in New York, and it was even our daughters' first time as well. As far as Quin, I think it was his second or third time because of his career. I felt so happy that my daughter was experiencing traveling at such a young age and to New York at that! She was only six years old then and I loved sharing this first-time experience with her. The four of us enjoyed our time but I didn't know my life would be close to ending following this trip. This is why I speak on enjoying life and for you not to ever get too high when things are great in your life. Also, never get too low when things aren't going so well. You don't want to live with fear or with too much caution but know that valleys will inevitably appear. You can't get to the mountain top without first going through the valley. I ended the year 2014 on a high note and my aspirations and positive mindset towards 2015 was at an all-time high. I felt that I was surely on my way to a mountain top in my life. This part of the story is important because life is full of peaks and valleys, you must enjoy it now because you never know what is awaiting around the next corner of life.

A Blessing in Disguise

I have a son named Devin. At the time of this story, Devin was 26 years old. Devin is a smart, articulate, and charming young man. I'm very proud of him and love him very much. He's my first born.

He followed after me in that he has always been a very good athlete too. Ok, I'll give his mother some credit too; she was a very good athlete in her day as well. Devin has always had the tools to be a success in life and it's great to watch him finding and following his passion. He looks like an Adonis, the handsome youth in Greek mythology. Devin is also a personal trainer therefore; he's very much into health and fitness. With that said, like all of us, Devin has also had his share of challenges in his life. He's seen some valleys in his life but I'm so proud to see him use those moments to propel him to become the great young man he is today.

Following this trip to New York, I began to hear from Devin on a more consistent basis. Almost weekly instead of the usual monthly. We had some great conversations and I really enjoyed them. I can recall one of the best conversations that Devin and I had. It was on one of my longest drives for my career in pharmaceutical sales. North Los Angeles to Monterey, California. During this drive, I had made a few stops on the way and there was a moment he caught me at the perfect time to listen and talk.

I enjoyed Devin telling me about certain books he was reading. I'd just relax and listen and marvel at his excitement about topics. Most of them were in the realm of personal development, which is near and dear to my heart. We went back and forth sharing mental notes about certain books, thoughts, and the takeaways. It was nice. Then suddenly, there was a short pause.

"Hey Dad can I ask you a question?" asked Devin.

"Sure son," I replied.

"Can I come stay with you for a little while?" he asked.

You see, at that time, Devin had never lived with me on a full-time basis. I was still in high school when he was born. Seventeen to be exact. And as promising as those times were for me, I had some tumultuous moments too. Living through teenage pregnancy was the most tumultuous of them all. For various reasons, his mother and I didn't stay together. We grew apart.

I ended up going away to college, and believe it or not, I had another child at the age of 20, with another woman! Oh yes folks, I have a story to tell. I've been through some things. I'll share more about all that throughout the book.

Let's get back to Devin and his request to come live with me.

After a short pause and a little shock, I said, *"Sure you can son. No problem. I have plenty of space."*

I lived alone in a large home with a couple of available bedroom so him coming to live with me wasn't a problem at all. Devin shared with me the reason he wanted to come stay and I was happy to accept him into my home. "Mi casa es su casa," I said with a laugh. He then told me that he expected to move in with me mid-February.

"Ok man, love you Pops," he said.

I replied, *"Love you too bro. Talk to you soon."* Then we hung up.

Even though we had never lived together up to this point, we've always had a good father-son relationship. I supported all of his endeavors be it sports, academics, and even a short stint he had in theater. As he grew into manhood we continued a solid relationship. I'll admit, I wish the relationship was better at the time but I'd still say it was good and respectful both ways.

Now the plot thickens! As they say.

A new year rolls around. Twenty-fifteen! I was excited about the new opportunity to do better this year, prosper, and grow in every area of my life. I placed my new goals on several walls in my house. I even listed my Vision 2020 goals. I was really motivated to make life happen at the next level. Also, my 44th birthday was approaching. January 19th, the best day of the year! I really consider that day the beginning of the New Year for me. As always, I was excited for the day and these were good times in my life. I was in a good place. Then, a few days before my birthday my cell phone rings. It was Devin. I figured he was calling to tell me early happy birthday, exchange pleasantries, and share more great development milestones for himself.

After a few minutes of conversation, he informed me that he'd like to move in with me sooner than later. **He anticipated late**

January instead instead of mid-February. I told him that it wasn't a problem. I was also thinking that I need to make sure that the room was ready for him sooner than later as well. **For me, thank God is was sooner!**

Post Strokes 2015

Terrance "Miracle" Minnoy

two days post stroke

me + taylor

learning to walk

...i can do it!

learning balance

practice makes perfect

keeping the fight

ct scan

THE STROKES

Terrance Minnoy   •••
February 9, 2015 at 6:50pm · 👥

"Now you out here all by yourself, ask Steve Jobs, WEALTH don't buy HEALTH!" - Pusha T. (Rapper) Through all the bravado comes wisdom in rap sometime LOL #HealthB4Wealth #FaithFamilyHealthFinanceFun #InThatOrder #TNV4LIFE

(Facebook post – 2 hours before first stroke)

I'm showing you my last Facebook post prior to my first stroke. Hindsight, I found it ironic that I'd be so moved by these rap lyrics that I found myself posting about it. As you can see, it had to do with the importance of good health. Wealth doesn't matter if you don't have good health. I was working at the time...building my wealth if you will. I soon would experience the overwhelming need for good health. This speaks to a subject I touch on in a chapter called The Universe Talks to You. Keep reading.

On the evening of February 9th I met with a good friend, Cicely, in north Los Angeles for a post-birthday dinner. We chose to do some shopping prior to having dinner. We were having a few discussions on various topics as we strolled through the halls of retailers. I was feeling great. As a matter of fact, prior to meeting up with her I had a good workout at my hotel. I even took a nap that evening. I felt fresh and vibrant.

And then it happened. Suddenly.

"What's the matter?" she said as I stopped walking and stood in place with a hand on my head. (Stroke #1, the TIA)
"I'm not sure but I need to sit down now," I replied.

I sat on a bench in front of Bloomingdale's. After sitting there and rubbing my head for a couple of minutes, I opened my eyes. I noticed something strange. Not only was my energy drained but I also couldn't read the Bloomingdale store sign without scrolling completely from the beginning to the end of the word. I recovered somewhat and we soon entered a shoe store to do some browsing. I saw Cicely speaking to a customer service representative in the store. It was later in the evening and slow in the mall so I assumed it was just us three in the store at the time. I was approximately fifteen yards away from them at the time and then I hear:

"I believe we have that size in the back." It was another female voice.

I was confused because it wasn't the voice of either my friend or the customer service representative she was working with. I moved my head slightly to the right and to my surprise, there she was. There was a second customer service representative in the store standing to the immediate right of my friend. Even though I was looking directly at my friend, I couldn't see this other person or objects to her immediate right unless I scanned to the right. Quite frankly, this disturbed me. It was later discovered that this was a right eye blind spot developed by the TIA.

The night continued.

We eventually went to dinner. While eating dinner, again, I had another episode of missing an object due to this blind spot. I thought I was done eating the orange chicken on my plate only to be directed that I had another piece I hadn't consumed...to the immediate right.

"That's weird." I said. We both laughed it off.

We soon ended our time together. I wanted to get to my room and get some sleep. I was surprisingly exhausted and I thought that I simply just need to get some sleep.

I slept deeply that night but I didn't feel completely refreshed. I still felt a slight headache and I knew that my vision was a little off. I texted Richard, my boss.

"I'm having issues with my eyes and I'm going to head home."

Home was about 90 minutes away. I was in north Los Angeles at the time and I live in Bakersfield. Through my primary care physician I already had an appointment scheduled with an eye doctor, Dr. Alexandrakis. I still noticed the problem with my eye on the drive but I made it to Bakersfield. In hindsight, I was very fortunate to make it to Bakersfield. I immediately went to his office. This was my first time seeing him so I had to fill out all the new patient information. After about an hour, I was called back to see the doctor.

"Hello, nice to meet you. What brings you in?" He kindly asked.

I commenced to tell him what happened the night before and that I was quite alarmed. I was so alarmed by it that I decided to be examined immediately. He proceeded to ask questions about my medical history and coached me through a battery of vision test. During our discussion about my medical history, I told him that I had a bout with Bell's palsy back in May 2013 which affected the right side of my face. My facial function was about 95% on the right side and then he took a close look at my face and said, "Oh yes, I can see some lingering effects." Once the examination was done he told me that I passed all the tests with flying colors and that my vision was good. I curiously looked at him. And then he said this. I will never forget:

"Terrance, you're a young man. You're very active. You don't smoke or drink excessively. You live a healthy and quiet lifestyle. But yet you had this bout with Bell's palsy a couple of years ago. If

I were you I'd get a CAT scan or an MRI, soon. Added that you are now having this vision issue, maybe something is going on in your brain. You should take a look."

I said, *"Ok Doctor, I sure will."*

I told myself that I'd go get it done in the next week or two.

Before heading home I ran a couple errands. I also went to get some "comfort food". That day it was chocolate cake from Jake's Tex Mex. It was delicious! I took some Advil and laid in my bed to decompress.

Then it happened.

About an hour after laying down to rest I noticed the room began to spin. I tried to raise myself up out of bed but my left arm was uncontrollable. I felt tingles throughout my body. I somehow made my way to the edge of my bed and tried to use the wall as leverage to stand up. I couldn't stand. Eventually I found myself on the floor. I couldn't raise myself up. I struggled attempting to do so. Soon, I felt something I was a little familiar with...a facial droop. I felt my face contorting and my words beginning to slur. I said to myself, "I think I'm having a stroke." I was very calm but I was afraid of course. (Stroke #2)

I wasn't sure if my son was home but I yelled his name as I laid on the floor of my bedroom.

"Devin, Devin, Devin!" I yelled at the top of my lungs. To my delight and surprise he came bursting into my bedroom.

"What's the matter Dad?" he said with panic in his voice.

"I think I'm having a stroke son. Call 911!"

Devin called 911. In the meantime, he kneeled near me to comfort me. As I remained on the floor, face first, I gave him my phone and ask him to call a couple of people immediately. I had him call Jennifer, my daughter's mother and Richard, my boss at work. Two things were of importance to me at that time. First, my daughter Taylor who was with Jennifer. Second, ensuring that my manager knew why he wouldn't be hearing from me any time soon.

Soon, the EMT showed up to my home. I'll never forget one of them, Chris. We've become friends since then. I really appreciated his attentiveness and assuring me that I would be ok. They followed all the procedures and had me at a top ranked stroke hospital within 30 minutes. I was rapidly moved through the emergency department and examined. Through comic relief, the presiding doctor on duty made me feel relaxed and confirmed that indeed I had a stroke. I was totally shocked and almost mortified but I was encouraged that I still had a little control of my left side. Unfortunately, there was more to come for me.

A few minutes after the doctor examined me I sat and waited patiently to be admitted. Jennifer and Devin were in the room with me at this time. A nurse entered the room.

"Do you have a Last Will or healthcare directive?" she kindly asked.

I replied, *"Yes."*

"Great, then can you sign this hospital waiver stating that you do have these documents."

She handed me a pen and placed the clipboard bound paper in front of me. Then, something went terribly wrong. I was holding the pen and attempting to sign my name on the paper. Even though I'm right-handed and the strokes affected my left side, I couldn't control the pen for some reason.

"Jen, I can't do it. I can't control the..."

I felt my body coil as if I was having a seizure. I got cold and shivers ran through me. I couldn't see anything but I could hear everything.

"Oh my God, someone please help him!" Jen screamed hysterically.

I could hear the nurse calming her. After about 15 seconds the episode stopped. This time though, my left side was completely immobile. I was drained. I wanted to fall asleep right away. (Stroke #3)

I won't bore you with all of the details of my months of care and rehabilitation following that day. I'll leave that for another book. Just know that following the third stroke I felt like I was surely going to die in the hospital that night. Nonetheless, I wasn't afraid. I was ready to embrace death. Maybe that's why at this time it's so easy for me to embrace life's adversities as they come. I feel that if I can survive that, I can survive anything!

In closing, I called this chapter; Timing is Everything - Devin, for a specific reason. First of all, it's really true, timing is everything. Secondly, things happen in your life, good and bad, for a reason. They all happen when they are supposed to happen. It may seem like happenstance or coincidence when things happen but I actually believe they are preordained moments. I know this may sound crazy to some of you but this is what I believe. God has planned every step in your life. He allows free-will; therefore, he also allows the byproduct of free-will which are those not so good moments in life. Things like mass shootings, deadly accidents, war, divorce, kidnappings, and even near-death experiences are like having three strokes in a 24 hour period. This section wasn't my "preach on a soap box" moment but I wanted you to know, believer or not, that your life has been orchestrated and planned by a higher power with the best of intentions for your life.

Devin had never lived with me full-time, yet at the age of 26, he came to do so. I had been living alone in that house for quite a few years. Obviously, normally I'm there all alone. He was suppose to move in with me in late February but things changed for him and he moved in January 25th, 2015...just two weeks prior to me having the strokes. If he hadn't been there at my home, at that particular time, I likely wouldn't be here today and you wouldn't be reading this miraculous story. I hope you're getting this! God is in control.

LET'S DISCUSS STROKE

I want to take time in this chapter to talk about stroke. Being that I had a stroke I think it's only appropriate that I take time in this book to talk about strokes. I'd be doing a disservice to the past, present, and future stroke victims and survivors if I didn't.

A stroke is a brain attack. There are two types of strokes that a person can have. It's when the flow of blood to the brain is cut off for a period of time due to a blood clot. That's known as an ischemic stroke. When a blood vessel in the brain burst, this is called a hemorrhage stroke. I had an ischemic stroke back in 2015. A blood clot settled in my brain stem then broke up into pieces. These pieces then settled in different parts of my brain which lead me to having multiple strokes.

Here are some statistics about strokes:

- **800,000 strokes in the United States every year**
- **Every 40 seconds someone has a stroke**
- **5th leading cause of death in America**
- **Every 4 minutes someone dies after having a stroke in America**
- **Leading cause of adult disability**
- **Strokes costs the United States an estimated 34 billion per year**
- **About 87% of all strokes are ischemic strokes**
- **80% of strokes can be prevented**

This is a good thing! There are choices we can make to significantly reduce the risk of stroke.

There are 10 risk factors to stroke:

1. **Prior stroke/TIA**. A TIA is a Transient Ischemic Attack. This is also known as a warning stroke. I had one of these. If you have a TIA there is a chance that you are going to have a stroke later. For me, that's exactly what happened. Within 24 hours I had a debilitating stroke.

2. **Hypertension**. This is known as the silent killer. We must manage our blood pressure.

3. **Myocardial Infarction**. A heart attack.

4. **Diabetes**. Blood sugars are too high. It's estimated that 30-40 million people have diabetes in the U.S

5. **Atrial Fibrillation.** This is the pooling of blood in a heart chamber due to an irregular heart beat. This develops a clot that eventually travels to the brain.

6. **Hyperlipidemia**. An increase in cholesterol.

7. **Carotid Artery Disease**. The hardening of the two main blood vessels that supply blood to the brain.

8. **Smoking**

9. **Excessive alcohol**

10. **Heredity**. The propensity for stroke can be passed through generations.

You may witness someone having a stroke. There is an acronym to help us recognize if someone is indeed having a stroke. That acronym is **F. A. S. T.**

F is for <u>FACIAL DROOPING</u>

A is for <u>ARM WEAKNESS</u>

S is for <u>SPEECH DIFFICULTY</u>

T is for <u>TIME TO CALL EMERGENCY SERVICES</u>

Anyone can have a stroke. It doesn't matter what age you are or your physical fitness level. I was totally shocked when my strokes happened. That was the biggest "curveball" that was thrown at me in my life to date. I don't like to see or hear of anyone suffering from a stroke but it's a part of life. Strokes happen all the time. There is nothing we can do about it. We should do our best to become a more aware, physically active, and a health conscious society.

I want to transition to a topic that I believe everyone is very familiar with. I believe that the statement I'm about to make is one of the realest statements in this entire book. The statement is as follows, **"Everyone has HAD a stroke of some kind in their life! As a matter of fact, everyone has likely had multiple strokes."**

EVERYONE HAS STROKES

In the medical sense, I've had experience with an actual stroke. Remember, stroke is defined as a **brain attack**. I've also had attacks in other areas of my life as well. I've had mental attacks. I've had spiritual attacks. I've had emotional attacks. I've had attacks in my relationships. Family attacks. Career attacks. Business attacks. Financial attacks as well. Anybody familiar? I'm willing to bet that if you're reading this book right now, you've had a stroke or several strokes of some kind in your life as well. Every area of our life is susceptible to having a stroke. In my case, unfortunately, some of these attacks were self inflicted. I was actually the cause of the attack. If I didn't cause it I surely played a role. I was basically attacking myself. Have you ever attacked yourself? Let's talk about it. How do you attack yourself?

1. **MAKING DECISIONS FOR SELFISH REASONS.**
   I've done this a few times in multiple areas of my life. I've

done it in my spiritual walk, my relationships, my career, and more. At times we look out for just ourselves or immediate gratification. We just can't be satisfied with our own lot or satisfied with what we have been blessed to have. We are always seeking more to the detriment of our well-being, integrity, and conscious. There is nothing wrong with striving to attain your goals and high achievement but we have to be careful in order to preserve our mental sanity, physical well being, and the ideal of never hurting someone else in the pursuit of greatness.

2. **CARING TOO MUCH ABOUT WHAT OTHER PEOPLE THINK ABOUT US.** Some of us will go so far as to living a lie in order to be accepted by others. Some people will do whatever it takes to be perceived by others as successful, flawless, and on the move in life. By purchasing things we can't afford, placing our children in certain schools, or falsely representing ourselves to gain favor, we are in hope of gaining the praise and respect of others.

3. **MINIMALIZING THE SUCCESS OF OTHERS.** Jealousy and envy may be the cause. This jealousy and envy may be subtle. Subconscious and involuntary movements or thoughts are usually involved. Which means you may not even be aware that you're minimizing another

person's success. Certain language may be used when it comes to certain people in an effort to "dim their light". When we attempt to take away or not acknowledge another person's success (inwardly or outwardly), we are attacking ourselves. We are taking a detour on the road to our own dreams and success.

Realize that we can attack ourselves intentionally or unintentionally by making involuntary and subconscious gestures of indifference towards another person. It's important that we look into the mirror and be realistic about this fact. Another reason it's important is that when we "keep it real" with ourselves we attract the good things that we want in life. We attract favor, healing, resilience, endurance, and enthusiasm when the chips are down for us. We become indifferent to the process of growth and overcoming hardships that are sure to come in our lives. When we take the time to do right by others it, in turn, serves us in the long run. Take some time to think about it and understand that you have strokes in different areas of your life. The important thing is this, how do you overcome the strokes. How do you recover from the divorce? How do you recover from the layoff?

The illness? The drop in sales? The slow down of business? The losses on the field or court? The death in the family? How do you recover from financial loss or credit card debt? Maybe the pain was self-inflicted. In your relationship you didn't live up to your own expectation let alone the expectations of your significant other. It's important that you find a way to bounce back from these situations. These attacks that we have in our lives. Here's a key thing that I learned from my actual stroke. Since I was off work for almost a year I had lots of time to think. I spoke quite a bit to friends, family, mentors, and confidants. I came to this realization. I've had many strokes in my life prior to this actual stroke. I got through those but I knew this one may be a lot harder to recover from. Then I realized I had already had practice with the recovery process because I had done it so many times before. What I'm saying is that my indifference to the recovery process following various strokes in my life actually helped me in my recovery process from an actual physical stroke. Here is a list of other strokes that happened in my life prior to February 2015:

- **Challenges of growing up poor**
- **Never having a father in my life - He passed before I was born**
- **Treated as a "black sheep" in my adolescence**
- **Breaking bones numerous times as a youth**
- **Losing friends to gun violence and drugs during my adolescence**
- **Becoming a teenage father (two children by age 20. Two different women)**
- **Giving up my son for adoption at birth (he found me when he turned 17)**

- **Being exposed and partaking in adult behaviors as a young teen**
- **Changing colleges following my freshman year**
- **Getting fired from a couple jobs as a youth**
- **Death of family members, in particular my biological mother, my brothers, and my aunt who raised me, Dorothy Coleman**
- **Setbacks and a couple reprimands in my career**
- **Lack of judgment and selfishness in various situations that harmed me**
- **Loss of friendships and numerous arguments**
- **My daughter's temporary placement in a school to help children with special needs**

You have the power, the resilience, the ingenuity, and the endurance to overcome any setback, stroke, or obstacle in your life from this moment forward. Why? Because you've likely dealt with some tough moments in your past. My hope is that you took copious, mental or written, notes about your experience in overcoming. I'm confident in saying that I believe 80% of the adversity we have in our lives are overcome using the same formula again and again. Think about your life. Look back at what you've come through. When you breakdown your recovery process in each setback, you'll likely see some similarities in the steps you took to bounce back. You likely got to the point of indifference to the stroke recovery process.

DECISIONS

Don't take decision making lightly. Here's what I mean. Every decision that we make in our lives matter. Our decisions and the actions we take following them, affect the remainder of our lives. Even the decisions we made concerning the small burdens we had at the age of fifteen has affected where we are today and possibly where we will be at age seventy. The decisions about who to hang out with and what functions to attend when you were in high school or college has played a role in your current situation. What books you decide to read and what TV shows you decide to spend time watching, affects you. Everything that you do, every decision that you make, matters. They really matter the most when we have those pivotal and future altering moments in our lives. I believe every person has **five to ten monumental and future altering moments in their lifetime**. All of these monumental moments won't always be good moments at first but they will be life changing when they happen. Many of them will happen, time will pass, and you'll forget about some of them because they happened so long ago. But when you sit down and really think about your life, and think about where you want to go, and think about your success or your lack of success, and think about what your true purpose is in this life, this is what you'll do. You'll reflect back to those moments and decisions you made. You'll reflect on them when you find yourself in the position to serve somebody else by sharing your story. When it's time to give a speech or to write something of importance, you'll start flashing back to those moments.

I can remember decisions that I made as a teenager that affect me today in my late forties. I made decisions regarding who I hung out with and what type of energy I wanted to exude. It was a decision I had to make because I grew up in an environment that, for most people, it dictated the decisions that you made and it dictated the energy that you exuded as a person. In high school, my basketball coach, Joe Dominguez, would always call me a politician. He'd say, "Minnoy you're a politician!"What's funny is that even back then as a teenager I took that as a compliment. To me, he was saying that I exuded good energy, I connected with others well, and that I was a leader. Maybe he was speaking into my future. Who knows? Since graduating college, I've been in sales. In some respect, using many of the same attributes a politician uses to get votes or earn the trust of his or her constituents. Like a politician, I work to transfer my beliefs on to someone else. I still receive it as a compliment to this day. As a teen, I exuded an energy of joy, of possibilities, of things getting better, and that I had the power to help and make things better. Coach Joe called me that because on the basketball court I was a politician with the referees. When calls were made for or against us I'd try to "work" the referee for future favor. (On a side note, I ironically became a basketball referee) I was a leader on and off the court. I would sometimes lead team meetings and try to inspire the team. Coaches and other men I respected at that time saw these attributes in me and they nourished it. I'm forever grateful.

I grew up on the eastside of Bakersfield, California back in the mid-80s. This environment back then didn't always lead to positive outcomes. It was gang infested. The crack epidemic had come along about then. We dealt with police brutality, high rates of teenage pregnancy, and poverty. You see, this environment didn't dictate a person having the type of energy that would have them called a politician...in a positive way. Eventually I was voted to be Student Body President of the school and the Homecoming King. You see, my environment did not dictate that happening but something was in me. This same something is in everybody else that wants more out of life.

I knew that I wanted to become more at a very young age. I call the something that's inside, our **light**. Everyone has a light. Not everybody has the courage to let their light shine. Either they don't have the courage or they're simply not given the venue to do so. I'm of the mindset that everyone should unapologetically let their light shine bright like a diamond.

I made the decision to not get enveloped in everything that was going on in my environment as a teenager. I was involved with my community but I didn't get enveloped in the wiles of my community (gangs and drugs). No, I wasn't perfect but I made a decision, regardless of what my friends thought about me. I kept a big smile, and to some people's displeasure, I hung out with people of the opposite race. I decided to be involved in community projects because a counselor at school saw something in me and wanted me to be a part of it. I'd speak to the kids at local junior high schools or the juvenile detention center. I was chosen to do those things. Even coming from my neighborhood, my light shined because I made a decision to let it shine unapologetically. I embrace it. You should do the same with your light. Those decisions that I made put me in a blessed place in life...where I am today. More importantly, those decisions that I made played a major role in me overcoming the handful of life changing moments that happened in my life. There are some decisions that I made back in high school that have affected me to this day when it comes to relationships. There are things that I did and decisions I made as a youth that weren't good. I got involved in some things that I shouldn't have got involved in. By God's grace I'm still here to tell you about it. Those decisions, I'm still reeling from. I'm still trying to overcome some "stinking thinking" due to some decisions that I made back when I was 15 years old. There are certain television shows that I decided to watch and people I decided to be involved with 30 years ago that have affected my position in society today. You see, I believe there is a lot more for me. I'm sure many of you feel the same about yourselves. I've been blessed to live a quality lifestyle but I truly feel that if I had made better decisions or went left instead of right 30 years ago, that I might be in an even better place today, possibly. I believe that professionally I would be in a different place. I believe that relationship-wise I would be in a different place. That place can be good or bad. I just feel that I made some decisions that set me back. Have you ever felt that way? Look, we have to be real with ourselves. That's so important. We must be honest with ourselves and occasionally look back at some of our decisions. I'm not telling you to look back with regret but sometime we have to look into the mirror and say, *"If I hadn't done* _____ *I would be* _____*."* Self confrontation and healthy reflection is a good thing.

- "If I would have joined the Chess club..."
- "If I would have decided to join the basketball team..."
- "If I would have practiced a little bit harder..."
- "I wish I would have studied more..."
- "I wish I would have gone on that camping trip..."

Teenager - Adult Decision

A decision that I made when I was in high school, age 17, I had my first child. That was a big decision for us to go through with the pregnancy. I was scared, I was afraid of what my mother would say. More so, I was afraid of what people would say about me. Nonetheless, we decided to go through with the pregnancy. Along comes Devin! The same Devin who'd play a role in saving my life twenty-seven years later. Have I said it enough? **Decisions that you make, matter!**

College Decision

At the time Devin was born I was a decent high school basketball player being recruited by a few colleges. I had a big decision to make. I can remember the final few schools that were aggressively recruiting me when the signing date came around. The schools were Idaho State University (ISU), University of San Diego (USD), Humboldt State, and UC Davis. I decided to go to Idaho State University for various reasons. I was really interested in University of San Diego but I hadn't heard from them for a couple weeks. I assumed they had landed the players that they needed and wanted. Idaho State made me feel like I was special and wanted. Ironically, on the very day of signing my letter-of-intent to attend Idaho State, I received a phone call from the University of San Diego. I remember it so well. Coach Barry

Janusch from ISU, my mother, and I were sitting in my living room preparing to sign on the dotted line. The phone rang. At the last minute, USD called offering me a full scholarship as well.

"Terrance, how are you? This is Coach from the University of San Diego."

"I'm doing well Coach. I hope the same for you," I replied.

"Terrance we want to offer you a full-ride scholarship to the University of San Diego," he enthusiastically stated.

(I paused.) *"Thank you coach but I'm about to sign with Idaho State as we speak."*

"Oh is that right?, he replied.

We ended the conversation with him saying:

"Terrance good luck in Idaho. I wish you the best and make sure you earn your degree up there."

"Thank you coach. Best of luck to you as well."

Decisions.

I went to Idaho State the following fall. After my freshman year, the coaching staff was fired. We didn't have a very good season. We went 6-21 to be exact. With lots of thought, I made the decision to transfer schools. Before looking at other Division I schools, at the behest of one of my assistant coaches, Coach Jeff Hironaka, I took a look at a small college in the Los Angeles area, The Master's University. He was going to be a new assistant coach at Master's University. After much thought and prayer, I decided to attend the school. **One of the best decisions I've ever made in my life!** I ended up having a very good basketball career. To make things even better, they honored my full scholarship until I graduated. It took me an additional year to graduate due to the transfer. I'm forever thankful for that. They allowed me to continue school, on their dime, even though my playing career was over! I got my B.S degree which catapulted me into corporate America success in sales and a great start to success in my life. I'm glad that I stuck with my decision to go to Idaho State University which in turn lead me to the Master's University. Who knows what would have happened if I had changed my mind and went to the University of San Diego. **Things happen the way that they are supposed to happen. I urge you, don't discount decisions that you make in your life. Big and small decisions can end up being equally important in the bigger scheme of things.**

I'll end this chapter by sharing one more monumental and pivotal decisions I had to make in my life. This is by far the most difficult decision I've ever made. This decision was life transforming, character building, and heartbreaking.

Dorothy L. Coleman – Decision

I was raised by Dorothy Coleman. Biologically she is my aunt. To me, she was my mother. She was the one that I called, "Momma". At the age of 2 my biological mother gave me to my aunt because she was trying to cope with life. Likely she was very stressed out. This stay with my aunt was supposed to be temporary. My biological mother was dealing with the anguish of losing my father, Fred Minnoy. My father passed away 4 months before I was born. I'm sure that before she came to the decision to leave me with my aunt, life was very tough on her. Not to mention, she had my two older brothers to raise. Keep in mind that my Aunt Dorothy didn't have children of her own. She actually never had a biological child. She raised me, she disciplined me, she fed me, and she clothed me. I was her child. Everything that a parent would do for a child, that's what she did for me. That was my mother, Dorothy Linda Coleman.

She had been a smoker most of her life, but in the mid-90s, she decided to give up smoking. Nonetheless, her weight remained an issue for her. She was overweight, and a diabetic along with a few other complications. Despite it all, she was a happy lady. As she got older, like many, she had her challenges. By the time 2009 rolled around she had been using a motorized chair for about 3 years. Due to the weight and other medical conditions, her knees were not functioning well. In the summer of that year, she developed an irritating sore on her abdomen. She was taken to the hospital where they admitted her. We assumed she'd soon be going home following the good care she was receiving. Unfortunately, while there she contracted an infection. The infection entered her body through her wound and within a day or so she was placed in ICU. All of a sudden, she was fighting for her life. Eventually, this lead her to being placed on life support. Her life weighed in the balance. She would get a little better and then a little worse. This continued for a couple days. She was slowly slipping away. And then this happened. The doctors and nurses came to me and said, *"Terrance, you have to make a decision. You have to decide if we should remove your mother from life support and allow her to pass."* What a decision I had to make. By now I was 38 years old. My mother was a devout Christian woman. She was looking forward to being with her Lord one day. So, I made a decision on behalf of my loving mother. On August 23rd, 2009 I allowed the hospital to remove life support machines from my mother. Within minutes, she passed away.

I feel like she was okay with my decision to let her go. When I think of that moment I sometimes wish I had did a few things differently. Hopefully, she and I can discuss it one day.

I made a very tough decision. Maybe you've been in a similar situation. That was a character building decision for me. A very painful one. Making that decision in 2009 truly affected every decision that came my way following. That will forever affect every decision that I make in my personal life and even in business. I'm thankful for that decision and that process. I grew as a person, I grew as a man. It gave me more reason to try to make her proud.

Decisions matter. They will help make your life matter to others as well. These decisions that you make as an adolescent or even in your twenties will affect how you're seen in the boardroom. Decisions affect how you are seen as a business owner or a sales person. Your decisions will even affect how your children view you and the level of respect that your peers give you. Decisions matter. My goal everyday is to make better decisions. I'm aware that the seemingly smallest decision I make today can make a huge impact in my future. Good decision making is pivotal to every fabric of our lives. We should work hard to improve our decision making skills. Let's always stay mindful that our decision making can have an indelible affect on others as well.

THE UNIVERSE TALKS TO YOU

How many of you know that the universe will talk to you and it has talked to you throughout your entire life? In this chapter I'm going to give you just a few examples of the universe talking to me. Hopefully it in some way can serve you as well. It's important to know this because a lot of us go through life wondering why certain things happen. Sometime we wonder why we made certain decisions or why we didn't listen to our gut. Many times when we're in this position we think about a decision we made months ago or sometimes years ago. We know that if we could change the decision we would because it has affected our current situation and lifestyle. Realizing that every action that we take, or don't take, will surely affect our next step in life.

I truly believe in a higher power and that higher power has a plan for our lives. From my understanding, in biblical times God would sometime talk to us using a booming voice from the sky. These days, I believe he talks to us silently now. When things happen, some people call it a coincidence. I read somewhere that, **"coincidence is God's way of remaining anonymous".** He's talking to us in many of these situations.

When the universe talks to you it tells you what's going to happen or what could happen. There's almost no way to decipher perfectly what it's saying but it's talking to you when things happen in your life, or don't happen in your life. You just have to take some time to slow down and listen. Most of the time you don't necessarily get what the universe is saying until we have a monumental moment and we say, "Gosh darn it, that's why that happened last month," or "that's why that happened last year." We also say, "That happened because this was going to happen." I'm sure many of you know exactly what I'm talking about.

There are some things that are going to happen in your life, a monumental moment that is going to dictate and serve you years from now. Here's an easy example that I think most of you can relate to.

There was a time when I was fired from a job. Not technically "fired". Let me explain. It was my third job out of college. My first job was manager trainee at JCPenney. My second job was at Pepsi-Cola in sales. I had a good five years at Pepsi but it was time for a change. I eventually left the company and decided to work for a manufacturing company called Rieke Packaging. It was a huge increase in responsibility. I now was stepping into the world of an account executive. My territory for this company was the entire western United States. It spanned from California all the way up to Washington. I also had responsibility out in Arizona and Colorado. To make a long story short, I took the job for all the wrong reasons. Yes, I like my manager who hired me but I was attracted to the opportunity to travel and get a company car. Then there was the money. I was so excited. I was going to get a base salary of $55K! This was the year 2000. Back then, for a 29 year old that was a lot of money. I'll be honest, I learned my lesson. Boy did I learn! Never take a job solely for the money.

As the Territory Sales Executive for this company I wasn't very good. I thought I would be. It was clear that the industry just wasn't for me. I mean, I was good at building relationships with people, and I definitely tried my best, but I wasn't that great technically and this job required that of you. During this struggle, I met one of my "angels" in life. A relationship that was a divine connection if you ask me. His name was Wayne.

In life there will be a few angels that will come into your life or cross your path. They may be there temporarily and some life-long. Personally, I have about six of these angels.

After a couple of years trying to get the swing of the job, I had to be in Indiana for a sales meeting. The company was headquartered there. Prior to my last day at the meeting Wayne ask me to breakfast the following morning. I agreed. I was a little nervous and apprehensive because I knew I wasn't very good at the job. I thought it was possible that I could be fired.

The morning arrived. We sat down and had a great meal. As we continued conversation he begins to say the following:

"You know what Terrance, I like you. You have a great attitude but I don't see the fire for this job in you anymore. I don't see what I saw in the interviews."

I completely understood what he meant by that. I'm sure he saw the nervousness on my face. He continued:

"Terrance, I'm not going to fire you, but I am going to give you 60 days to find a new job."

I was confused but I was even more taken back with what he had said next.

"I'm going to pay you for the next 60 days. You don't have to come to work, but I'm going to continue to pay you your $55,000 salary for the next 60 days and during this time, I want you to find a new job that's for you."

Inside I was yelling, "WOW! Thank you Lord."

I returned home. A couple of weeks later I had to turn in the car and all the other perks that came with the job. The checks kept coming.

Now here's where the universe began to talk to me. Before I had taken this job I got involved in a home-based business called Pre-Paid Legal (now called LegalShield). I got involved because a number of my friends were doing it. I invested 2-4 hours/wk on my own time. Eventually my 60 days was up and the checks would soon stop. I remember it well. My last check arrived in late February 2003. Here's the kicker. Pay attention! One week later, I reached one of the top positions in Pre-Paid Legal! I now started making $3-5K/mo from home...part-time! I didn't share this story to brag or impress you. I shared to impress upon you that the universe will tell you when you're not in the right place or position. It will show you provision even when you don't deserve it sometime. See, God will allow you to go through some rough patches in your life. He will allow you to go through some tough experiences. He will also give you opportunities to grow as you journey into places you don't feel comfortable. I believe that's exactly what the job with Rieke was all about for me. The job was preparing me. Preparing for what? Preparing me for success in the network marketing industry. Success in my current career in pharmaceutical sales. And indeed, success in recovering from three strokes in 24 hours!

I have been in pharmaceutical sales for 12 years now. I have a very large territory. A company car. An expense account for company business. A favorable work schedule. I'm more than grateful for my career and company. I've had a very productive and fruitful career. If I hadn't gone through those tough years prior to pharmaceuticals, I wouldn't have been prepared to have the career I've had thus far. I also wouldn't have learned to hone the skills of team building and sales excellence that I learned in Pre-Paid Legal. Not to mention, I was introduced to the personal development industry through the network marketing industry. I find that much that I learned in that venture has paid dividends in my corporate America journey.

You will go through some tough moments. You will find yourself in uncomfortable positions on dead-end jobs or in unfulfilling relationship. You'll think, "This isn't good for me. How did I get here?" Years later you'll reflex back and say, "oooh that's why I went through that." This is the universe talking to you.

Here's another example of the universe talking to me.

I'm a sales/marketing professional by nature. It seems to be my "sweet spot". Nonetheless, I somehow found myself teaching special education. Yes, I was once a special education teacher. Prior to my career in pharmaceutical sales I taught special education for young adults between the ages of 18-22. I happened to be at the gym one day working out and ran into a good friend of mine from high school, Joey.

As we were catching up I told him that I was between jobs and currently building a business from home. He then mentioned that he was now a lead supervisor for a special education program through the high school district. Their program was in need of an additional teacher. He inquired if I'd be interested. He told me that he thought I'd be a great fit. I've never taught in a classroom before but my interest was piqued. He invited me to come take a look at the program.

I eventually checked out the program and I thought it was great. I felt comfortable in the environment. I like all children but there's a special place in my heart for children and adults who are handicapped or have mental disabilities. I've always had a soft spot for them.

These young adults had mental disabilities, mainly down syndrome. My role as their teacher was to teach them life skills like cooking, basic math skills, public transportation, how to get along in life, and how to help their caretakers serve them. I had a great time with that job. I truly enjoyed it. This job was one of the best jobs I ever had. To this day I'm thankful and filled with fond memories from that experience.

I grew close with some of the kids and their families. As a matter of fact, when a couple of the students past away, the family invited me to attend the funeral. I was honored. After a year or so, my time as a teacher came to an end. The pharmaceutical sales industry came calling.

As I stated before, sales is my sweet spot. This job was a better fit for me than teaching. Things happen for a reason. I can recall looking back and thinking, *"I wonder why God had me teaching special education for a couple of years?"* Why did the universe send me that way? Why did I have a pit stop as a teacher in special education?" I found out one reason some five years later.

My daughter Taylor was born in 2008. She was born six weeks early and she spent a few weeks in the NICU, following her birth. Within a year I noticed some oddities about her. Her mother couldn't tell but I could. Something definitely was different. Sometimes she'd crawl in an odd way (using the back of her hands instead of her palms). She'd rarely give us eye contact. She would rhythmically bounce off the back cushion of the couch while sitting. I knew, something wasn't right.

As Taylor got older and started developing she showed signs of being autistic. She wasn't functioning at her age level. Because I had the experience of being a special education teacher I recognized some of the signs that Taylor had some issues. I wouldn't have recognized anything that was wrong with my daughter if I hadn't taught special education for a little while. We were able to get Taylor some intervention right away because I noticed some signs that something wasn't right. We later learned that she isn't autistic but she was diagnosed with Auditory Processing Disorder. She has made great strides and caught up to grade level in many subjects. She is now 9 years old (at the time of this writing).

I'm so thankful that I had that experience as a special education teacher. It served me well with my daughter who was born several years later and have some developmental problems.

The universe will definitely talk to you. Pay attention and never take anything for granted.

Here's one last example of the universe talking to me.

Going back to my stroke episodes in 2015, the universe was speaking to me then. Approximately 10 months prior to the strokes, my boss introduced me to a young man named Nick, he met at a small group at his church. My boss and I would occasionally discuss finances, and ways to improve them. The young man he wanted me to meet, Nick, apparently worked in financial planning and he thought I should get some insights from him. Eventually we met over the phone. Following the initial conversation, we'd regularly have phone interviews so that he could learn more about me and my financial goals. His goal was to get to know me better in order to present beneficial information to me in the future. He was thorough in doing his homework. I really like that.

In December 2014, he presented a proposal to me. He offered me the life insurance policy that I wanted and at a reasonable price. He went on to offer me a disability policy, and I was thinking to myself, "I'm not sure I need that, I already have a disability policy through work." He went on to share the benefits of the policy. I was reluctant. Eventually I had a change of heart. Here's why: It's the end of the year and it's possible he has a sales goal for the year and I empathize with that. I'm in sales myself. Therefore, I agreed to the policy, thinking I'd never use it and I'd drop it in a year. **Remember, this was December 2014**.

Fast forward to February 9, 2015, just two months after signing the new policies, I suffered from 3 strokes in one day and I almost lost my life. Now here's the "wow" moment.

For the first 90 days that I was out of work my company paid me 100% of my salary. After 90 days, I'd only get paid 75% of my normal salary. By God's grace I was still able to live off 75% of my income, which came out to be $1000/month less in take-home pay. Well, remember the disability policy Nick encouraged me to purchase in December 2014? The policy I didn't feel I had a need for? This policy kicked in as well after my 90 days of being out of work. The amount of the policy? One-thousand dollars per month! The money I wasn't receiving from my job was supplemented by a policy I never thought I needed. **THIS WAS THE UNIVERSE TALKING TO ME!** I'm here to tell you that when the universe talks to you, listen! You have to be open-minded and understand that the decisions you make right now will affect how your life turns out years from today. You can call it a coincidence if you want, but I'm here to tell you that the universe will talk to you. Do you hear what I'm saying?

When it talks to you, it's telling you something of significance. At that moment we are oblivious to its signs and its speech. We don't understand it at all. I'm much more keen to those moments now. When things happen, when I run into someone unexpectedly, and when a seemingly insignificant idea or thought comes to mind, I make sure that I pay attention. Why? Because it can surely mean something of significance in my future. I truly believe God, the universe, talks to you. Listen.

DISCIPLINE YOUR DISAPPOINTMENT

As I've aged, I can't think of anything attained of any significance in life without pain. Life is hard. Get that in your head right now. **LIFE IS HARD!** You know what else is hard? Building a business. Building a relationship. I don't care how many great moments you have in life and I don't care how many great moments you have in your relationship, it's doggone hard. Raising a child is hard. Getting a promotion at work, in many cases, is very hard. Being a great mother or father is not easy. Even being a great friend is not always easy. It should be, but it's not. Life is forgiving but there are unapologetic and constant "blips" in life. I like to call these blips disturbances or storms. But lately I've called them **"strokes"**. Attacks. Rough patches. Tough spots. Rocky roads. These blips are a must. As a matter of fact, if you don't have these blips in your life it's possible that you're dead! If you don't have blips in pursuing your dreams then your dreams are likely dying. If you don't have blips in building your relationship, building your family, your career, your business, your social life... all of those things are dead or suffering a slow death. Think of a heart monitor. If a person's heart monitor flat-lines, this means whomever or whatever that heart monitor is connected to has no heartbeat and most likely it's dead. Now think about it when it comes to blips. Blips are actually good disturbances. Blips say that you are alive. Again, consider the heart monitor. When there are blips in the monitor, the indication line is going up and down. Sharp ascensions and dissensions means that person or thing is alive! You want your heart monitor to have blips in it when it gets connected to you. That means you're alive. It's a good thing. They are necessary. Disturbances in your life are necessary in order for you to live out your dreams and goals. If you want to change and evolve as a person, as a leader, as a parent, as a teammate, as a spouse... as tough as it may be at times, you have to embrace these disturbances. You also need to understand that they are here to help you. It's a signal that you're doing well in most cases. You are alive.

What do we do when these blips and disappointments occur? We have to learn to discipline ourselves in these moments. A mentor of mine once said, **"Learn to discipline your disappointments."** I've learned that there are techniques to disciplining your disappointment.

Here are a few:

1. **Following the initial shock or sting of a disappointment, you should first take a deep breath and be still.** Some people like to take this time to pray or meditate. Whatever you do, take time to relax if possible. Talk quietly to a friend or confidant. Don't overreact to the disappointment.

2. **Take a good look at yourself.** Be honest with yourself. Ask yourself is this something you saw coming based on your own behavior, decision making, and acceptance. Maybe it's a health matter that you could've addressed in a more preventive manner at some time in your life. Here's my personal example of that. At the time of the strokes I was doing many of the right things in life. I was working out consistently, I didn't smoke, and I didn't have high blood pressure. Bottom line, I was a very active person. I was only 44 years old. Nonetheless, I can think of a few things that maybe I could've modified. Considering that stroke,

diabetes, and heart attack ran prevalent in my family history, I should've been more vigilant in some areas of my health. As a matter of fact, just 4 months before I was born my father died of a massive heart attack. I've told by family members who knew my father that it wasn't his first heart attack. He's even had strokes in his medical history. It's also possible that I exacerbated things with my sugar intake, lack of sleep, and constant long drives in the car for my career in the pharmaceutical sales. I took some time in the hospital to take a good look at myself and my own behavior first.

3. **Face the challenge.** Address the setback head-on. You can't tippy-toe into it. For those who know stories in the Bible, you'll get this example. The story of David and Goliath. David was as shepherd boy. He was skilled with the slingshot but he wasn't known as a great warrior. Goliath was a nine-foot giant that challenged the Israelites to fight to the death. He taunted them. No one amongst the Israelites would take on the challenge. David soon

stepped up to the challenge. As Goliath continued taunting, David confidently shouted to Goliath, *"I'm going to cut off your head and feed it to the birds of the air!"* Goliath laughed at David. This was David's disappointment, his "stroke", his blip. **David approached Goliath with haste**, swiftly, without hesitation. He ran towards Goliath and slung his rock. The rock struck Goliath and killed him. This is what we should do when we face our obstacles, challenges, and setbacks. Run towards them and face them head-on!

4. **Forgive and evaluate.** Don't just forgive the offender. Forgive yourself! Especially if you played a role in the situation. If you didn't pay attention to the morale of your team and something goes awry within it, then you were at fault to an extent. If your relationship falls apart and you noticed prior signs of it doing so, yet did nothing, then it was partly your fault. Forgive yourself. The disappointment may not be your fault at all. Approve yourself. You may have been dealt a bad hand in life. Approve

yourself. Your child may have gone wayward in school or got into drugs. You missed the signs. If that's you, forgive yourself. Approve yourself but also give yourself permission to get better. Don't sulk. Learn from the situation and take actionable steps to get better.

Setbacks, challenges, and obstacles are necessary. That's just the way the world works. There's no getting around it. If you choose to stay in this world you are also accepting everything that comes with it. Understand, for the most part, there are going to be joyous and happy times in your life. But there are going to be moments of disruption. Before peace there is war. Before recovery there is usually a disturbance of some kind. I've miraculously recovered from my major disturbance. Before a mother gives birth there is lots of pain. Before winning there are usually hard lessons learned in losing first. Before that muscle gain or weight loss, there is strenuous and painful work that needs to happen first. Sometime, your friends start out as your enemy.

Let me share this story with you. As a youth, many of my best friends were my enemies at first. I can think of a good friend named Devon. We grew up together in the mid-80's. He and I became very close. We played on the same basketball teams growing up. We created rap music and wrote poetry together. We ran with the same crew. There was no doubt that we were close and cared for one another. Devon has always been a good dude.

Devon and I didn't start out that way. We met in Jr. High school. I was a popular guy in school. I had a chip on my shoulder. I thought I was tough. I was known as a good athlete and an overall good guy but I had my moments of mischief. To make a long story short, Devon was new to Compton Jr. High School in Bakersfield. He and his family were new to the town as well. I remember it like it was yesterday. We were in Mrs. Waterman's music class. I hadn't formally met Devon yet. It may have only been his first or second day at the school. His desk was right behind mine. When I'd sit in my desk I'd sometime bend my knees in a way that my feet would go back on both the right and left side. Devon was tall so when he would stretch his legs out, his feet would inevitably touch my feet. This irritated me a little but I made it worse because I was a little punk at the time. I wanted to let the new kid know that I was "the man". We exchanged some not-so-kind words and I soon turned around in my desk, looked him in the eyes, and, *"POW!"* I punched him in the nose as hard as I could. There was blood everywhere! I was taken to the office and later suspended from school for a week. That's how our relationship started. Enemies. Somehow we became the best of friends over time. Likely we connected through our love for rap music at that time. We don't talk much now but when we do it's heartfelt love.

I shared that story because in many situations, there is always chaos before the calm. Thank God for our chaos.

Before I had a great career in the pharmaceutical sales industry, and before I grew a successful business in multi-level marketing, I was fired from a couple of jobs. I can recall having medial summer jobs cleaning school desks and washing the walls of the school. It didn't feel good at all. Things seemed bleak. I now appreciate those moments. It led me to success in my career, business, and even served me with recovery from my strokes. Those experiences taught me great lessons. They toughened me and this is why you should **see failure and disappointment as flattery.** The universe wants you to be ready for your future greatness in various areas of your life. It's taken a moment out of its busy schedule to throw you a curveball. It threw you a curveball because it knew you could "knock it out the park". It knew you were going to use that situation to get better and make a mark on this world. You can use these situations like sandpaper. Use them to smooth out those rough edges in your own personality and eventually smooth out any rough spots that you deal with in life.

Prior to this book, prior to speaking engagements, interviews, branding, and accolades, I had three strokes in one day! My journey to become an author and speaker was birthed through disappointment, challenge, and setback. I embraced the adversity. I ask that you do the same. **Embrace adversity**.

Remember this, as soon as you declare to the universe that you are going to make a mark in this world like write that book, excel on that project, lose that weight, or build that business, that's when it will allow negative forces to test your word and commitment. Accept the challenge. You haven't flat-lined yet so you're more than capable of achieving your goals and dreams.

SPASTICITY

Saebo, Sept 9, 2015

Signe Brunnstrom (1898-1988) was a Swedish-American physiotherapist, scientist and educator. She is best known for her discovery on the sequence of stages of recovery from hemiplegia after stroke, which later came to be known as the Brunnstrom Approach. This approach was developed in the 1960. With seven stages, the Brunnstrom Approach breaks down how motor control can be restored throughout the body after suffering a stroke.

Stage 2 of this approach is called, <u>Dealing with the Appearance of Spasticity</u>. Spasticity is when muscles are continuously contracted. When I had my strokes, the left side of my body was affected. For a few weeks my left arm, hand, and fingers remained contracted. My fist remained balled. My arm was in a cocked position and close to my torso most of the time. I could move my shoulder a little but from my elbow down to my forearm and hand, it remained stiff. They call that spasticity. This happens because of the significant nerve damage in the affected limbs. Maybe you've seen this in people who have had traumatic brain injuries or a stroke. They walk with a continuous limp, limb drag, or have contracted muscles. Brunnstrom stated that spasticity decreases in about two-thirds of stroke patients. This happens due to normal nerve repair but the most important way that spasticity decreases is through therapy. This is the main reason that a few days after a stroke happens you start physical therapy. I can recall being in the hospital, barely able to move on my own. A therapist came to my room and did some therapy with me as I lay in bed. On a side note, the therapist that came to my room to work with me was a high school classmate, Freddie. How ironic! He encouraged me and spoke life into me. He kept reminiscing on our high school days and touted how great an athlete that I was. He said because of that I would bounce back strong from the strokes. He was so right! Even though I couldn't stand or move my arm, he would do it for me. He knew the importance of muscle memory and repetition.

It took about three weeks for the spasticity to decrease and I was able to do some of the movements myself. Eventually, I fully overcame spasticity.

Here's the reason I'm sharing spasticity with you.

Even now, three years post strokes and back to a full life as it was before, I still have subconscious involuntary episodes of spasticity. There are times when I'm doing things around my house and in public, I find myself not using my left arm or hand. I could easily do it but subconsciously I choose not to. I catch myself holding my left arm and hand in a position as if I still have spasticity. After laughing at myself, I quickly stretch my arm and hand out then commence to use it. To this day I make conscious efforts to use my left arm and hand more because subconsciously and involuntarily spasticity sets in.

My point is this. You may have made a great comeback in your life. You finally moved on from that draining relationship. You positively changed habits which in turn changed your behavior. You overcame that illness or recovered from that car accident. You found a new and better job after getting laid off several months ago. Yes! You've made great strides following your setback. You're feeling good about yourself and your future. Nonetheless, you're human and occasionally spasticity sets in. You will revert back to some of those old habits and ways of thinking. You'll get back in that toxic relationship. You'll go back to being an average sales representative after you had turned the corner to become a great sales representative. You'll fall back on your diet and fitness goals. Again, many times you'll do this subconsciously and on occasion, intentionally.

Many of the things that hold us back in life we revert back to because of our own bout with spasticity. We won't even recognize it sometime until after it happens. Our muscle memory and habits take us back to a place we don't want to be. We contract. Spasticity sets in. I could be just speaking for myself but in our spiritual walk we revert back instead living up to the standards we were taught as children growing up in church. In our career we revert back to some of the habits we had when we weren't successful. Supposedly, we turned the corner but yet subconsciously those bad habits will settle back in because of spasticity. In business, in our finances, and some of our spending habits we revert back to a time and place we don't want to be. It's because of spasticity in our finances.

So how do we overcome spasticity? I don't believe we ever fully overcome it in some respects. I say that because now, three years following the strokes, hundreds of workouts complete, thousands of repetitions, and many miles ran, I still find myself holding my arm and hand stuck in a position of spasticity. I usually glance at my arm and I'll say to myself, *"Terrance what are you doing?"* Then I commence to straightening my arm and then I'll use it the right away.

That's how you overcome the spasticity that is happening in your life. You're human, it's going to happen. You're not perfect. Sometime you'll contract and revert back when you should be moving forward. The important thing is what are you going to do about it?

Here are a few things that'll help you when you notice spasticity creeping into your life.

1. **Look at yourself.** Whenever I'm having a bout with spasticity, I'll immediately look at my arm and intentionally straighten it out. This has to happen when you see spasticity in your life. Look in the mirror and say, "yes I reverted back." Briefly deal with yourself and get back on the path that you want to be on in your life.

2. **Immediately practice the right behavior.** As I noted, whenever I subconsciously allow spasticity to happen with my left arm, I would start using it more than usual. I'll do everything with using my left hand. Practice, practice, practice. Know the correct result-driven behaviors and do them. Do the exact opposite that the spasticity would remind you to do. Get in some repetitions and improve your behavioral muscle memory.

3. **Approve yourself.** Don't get mad at yourself. Understand that you are not perfect and it's part of your process to move to the next level in life. Failure will happen. The key is to see failure as your friend. If you are making progress in life, 95% of the time, don't disregard your progress because of the 5% of the time you had a subconscious setback. Remember, you are not your mistakes!

You may temporarily, on occasion, revert back to an old mindset that doesn't serve you. You have to recognize it right away and change that behavior immediately. Understand that your resilience and greatness is strengthened by your intentional self confrontation and honest self evaluation. Spasticity doesn't always have to make its presence known in your life.

WANDERING GENERALITY
OR MEANINGFUL SPECIFIC

I recently began listening to the late great Zig Ziglar on a more consistent basis. If you're not familiar with Zig Ziglar I strongly suggest that you become familiar with him. He's a teacher and speaker in the world of sales. He's an expert at motivating people for sales excellence. Even though he touches on the sales industry most of the time, he does talk about life in general and gives some great advice.

A very insightful and thought provoking question he regularly asks is, *"Are you a wandering generality or a meaningful specific?"* When I first heard this question I immediately had to rewind the video. I thought it was a brilliant question to ask the audience. Then I had to ask myself, "Am I a wandering generality or a meaningful specific?" I'd like to say I'm surely a meaningful specific but I've had my moments of being a wandering generality. Maybe you've been at some point as well.

Let's discuss each for a moment.

It's tough to be effective, impactful or resilient if you're a wandering generality. Let me ask you a few questions. Are you just going through the motions of life? Are you working just hard enough that you don't get fired? Are you giving the best effort that you truly can during your workouts? Do you only motivate yourself and never encourage someone else? Do you pursue only average results? Are you ok with just "getting by?" Do you care to make an impact in someone's life? Is it "all about you?" Don't get me wrong, sometime it feels good to be a wandering generality or having a day of wandering generality. There are times that I don't want to be impactful, encouraging and resilient. The difference is that I eventually get uncomfortable being that way after a while. I'm wired to be a meaningful specific. When I leave this world I want people to know that I left. I want to make such an impact with my family, friends, and others around me that my energy and presence are noticeably missing. As Les Brown says, "I want to make a mark in this world. I want people to know that I was here." When you're a wandering generality, you don't care if you make a mark or not. You can care less if people notice your presence. You just want to get paid. You just want to "stay in your lane". If you're a wandering generality, in general, you tend to be a wandering spirit when a stroke/distractraction/blip happens in your life. You take a blow from life, take a knee, and never get up until the opponent leaves the ring or you're counted out. There's nothing wrong with "taking a knee" occasionally in life. We all need to gather ourselves at times. Reset! The key is to never stay down. It is your God given right to have high expectancy for success, recovery, and abundance. Being a wandering generality doesn't stir up the energy we need to overcome adversity and showcase our resilience. It doesn't attract favor. It doesn't attract healing, recovery, productivity, or positivity. If we want these things to be a constant in our lives then we must do our best to avoid being a wandering generality.

Let's discuss being a meaningful specific? What does it mean? A meaningful specific lives a life that's more mission driven than a wandering generality. These are mission and purpose driven individuals. No matter how the wind blows in their lives, the mission and purpose never changes. Usually the mission is tied to serving others in some type of way. They move with purpose. They move with energy. They move with focus. I'm not saying that they don't have fun and occasionally "let their hair down," but they even do that for a specific reason. That reason is to simply refuel for the mission at hand. Correctly assumed, being meaningful automatically means meaningful to someone or something else. Know this, your greatness, success, and impact in this world is always tied to someone else. It's never just about you. As soon as you fully believe in this statement the sooner you will overcome any stroke in your life, and the sooner you will achieve your dreams and goals. There are advantages to being a meaningful specific. Allow me to share some of them:

- **You achieve more in your family, career, and business**
- **You achieve more of your goals**
- **You are more resilient. You have bounce-back power**
- **You learn more from your mistakes and failures**
- **You attract favor into your life**
- **You tend to have a long-term vision and more consistent work ethic**
- **You can survive severe strokes and storms in your life**
- **You're looked upon as a leader and sought after as an expert**
- **You give others confidence and help them feel good about themselves**

I learned from the late Paul Meyer that when you are goal-setting, be sure to be specific. There is power in being specific. If you set a goal to get a new car by next Christmas, be specific about that car. What color? What model? What horsepower? What color interior? Hybrid or electric? Sedan or coupe? I can go on and on. The point is that being specific about any goal or mission is a must and works most of the time. Even if you don't hit your goal you'll likely be in a much better place than you were beforehand. You'll be in a higher state of existence, achievement, peace, and mind.

Les Brown says, "Shoot for the moon. Even if you miss, you'll still be amongst the stars."

STOP HUSTLING BACKWARD

I'll be the first to admit that I've done this before. Hustled backwards. For those who may not know the meaning of this phenomenon, here is one meaning directly from the Urban Dictionary:

"Busting your butt without making any progress."

Note that this lack of progress may be a result of how the system is set up. This lack could also be solely based on the decisions and actions of the participant. Usually when the term is used it's used in a business or business transaction sense.

For example, if someone is in the house flipping business, they purchase homes below market value, renovate/invest in them, and then put them up for sale. Yet, due to either the real estate market or negligence on their part, they end up selling the home for less than what they invested or for very minimal profit. That is what you call hustling backwards.

What I've learned in my life is that you can hustle backwards in various areas of your life. In this chapter I will give you a few examples of hustling backwards. Bottom line, you don't want to be a hustler that habitually hustles backwards. Going hard with no progress. Devaluing your time, products, and more importantly, your spirit.

I assume that most people know the term hustler. Today, being known as a hustler is a good thing. I can recall the days when being known as a "hustler" was actually a bad thing. Those were the days of the pimps and drug dealers hanging out on the corner. The neighborhood "no good man" was known as a hustler. He was the guy that would come by the house and sell various goods for cheap. We would always wonder where the stuff came from. The deal would be so good that you just couldn't pass it up.

Who remembers Hustle Man from the TV show Martin? Hustle Man was played by, Tracy Morgan. Hustle Man did it all! He had deals on just about everything. Be it food, flowers, car tires, or wedding planning services, Hustle Man could always hook you up. I laugh out loud even now as I'm writing. Some of those episodes were hilarious!

Here's a quick and realistic example of hustling backwards that most of you can relate to I'm sure. The treadmill. This is the prime example of hustling hard yet going nowhere...at least when it comes to location. I workout often. I'm not a huge fan of the treadmill but I like the burn of calories that it gives me. I also like the lather tends to build on our bodies when we are on the treadmill. I go hard but I know good and well that I'm not going to go anywhere. The treadmill isn't going to leave the building. Regardless of how hard I run, I will not leave that building while on the treadmill. That's hustling backwards. Again I'm not not knocking your regular treadmill workouts. They serve a purpose for sure. The point I'm making is that people run hard, try to make the right decisions, do the right thing yet in some respects, intentionally hustle backwards. I **intentionally** get on the treadmill at the gym knowing for a fact that I'm going to hustle hard...and go nowhere!

We do this in life as well. We do this in business, in our health and fitness, in our spiritual walk, in our relationships, and in our overall development as people. Let's discuss a few of these areas.

Business.

How do you hustle backwards in the business setting? Here are a few examples.

You work in an office setting. You work hard and diligent. You want to be seen in a positive light. You'd like to get promoted in the near future because you want to increase your income and acquire the other perks of promotion. You want to have an overall positive reputation for yourself and cement the trust of your leadership so that they consider you for future opportunities. This is all great! Yet, this is how you can hustle backwards in your efforts. You'll allow your personal dislike for someone in the office show on your face or become public knowledge throughout the office. Your interaction with your leadership isn't with energy that would have you stand out to them. Your energy doesn't set you apart. That's hustling backwards! You're an office complainer, gossiper, and known to be petty. Hustling backwards!

In the school setting, you had a month to get a project done and here you are pulling an all-nighter the night before just to get it done. I've been there before. That's hustling backwards. You knew that project was due a month ago but you waited.

In business you have to be careful to not hustle backwards. But strangely enough, most people don't know why they're not getting that promotion or not being as liked around the office. This is mainly because you might be hustling backwards.

In the business setting it is important to be a team player but there are times where you want to have the lead on a project or in the department. While in that position all you do is complain a lot which gives off bad energy. Soon people don't want to see you in that role because you lack the positivity it takes to lead a project or lead others.

Look, your job is to make positive moves. You want to be considered for upward mobility. You want to be known as a team player. You expressed that during your interview. Ninety-nine percent of people always say, "I'm a team player" during the interview process but don't act like one when they don't get their way or dislike someone. That's hustling backwards.

While working at a company, you might decide to start a "side" part-time business to supplement your income in order to serve your family. There is nothing wrong with this unless it conflicts with your current employment or takes time away for your corporate duties. However, instead of just working hard at your current company to build it, you spend company time trying to build your own business That's hustling backwards because how do you expect to have success outside of your job if you're not diligent in your current role at work?

You have to pursue excellence in your current situation if you want God to bless you in other ventures as well. If you're not doing so then you're hustling backwards.

Health & Finances.

Let's move onto another set of hustling backwards, health & fitness. I'll admit, it's easy to hustle backwards in this area. I workout quite a bit but I also snack on Oreos too much at times. We have this image of ourselves and who we want to be yet we don't take the necessary steps, on a consistent basis to achieve our image goals. We'll do it temporarily but we don't have the discipline to continue. Rest assured, I'm speaking of myself as well. We hustle backwards by fooling ourselves. We have good workout for a couple days then we hit up McDonalds thinking it's okay because we got it in those great workouts. That's hustling backwards. We know exactly what it takes for us to be successful when it comes to our health and fitness but we don't practice the patience and diligence it takes to achieve our goals. Understand, we didn't get out of shape overnight and we aren't going to get in shape overnight. The improvements will be gradual. We won't see the improvements for a little while. As a matter of fact, other's will likely see the improvements in you before you!

I get it, we all have our vices or guilty pleasures, our strongholds, and we are going to fall sometime. That's ok. As much as possible we want to avoid those intentional bad habits that cause us to hustle backwards.

Relationships.

You can hustle backwards when it comes to relationships and friendships. You want to attract a good partner into your life but you're not willing to make any type of changes that would make you more attractive (inside and out) to another person. Maybe you feel like you have it all already. I'm sure you look good and you have a great package but everything isn't for everybody and everybody isn't for everything. There may be some things you need to tweak a little bit. If you're having a problem finding a good and comparable mate you have to be open to changes or small tweaks. You have to work on you, first! If you're not working on yourself, you're hustling backwards! Look into the mirror. Be truthful and honest with yourself. You have to think about some of the things that you do and how you carry yourself. Are they conducive to attracting what you want in a partner? Are you pessimistic? Are you negative? Are you a complainer? If you're not doing a real personal assessment of yourself you're hustling backwards. If you're not willing to change or be flexible it's going to be tough to attract someone with those qualities.

You may be currently in a committed situation or married right now but you'd like to take the relationship to higher heights. In order to do so, your significant other needs to feel good about themselves and the relationship. It's your duty to help them with that. Therefore, don't forget to compliment them. Speak positivity and victory into them. Meditate and pray for them. Continue to do those things that attracted you to them...and even take it up a notch. If you're not willing to do some of these things, I must say, you're hustling backwards!

I think you get the message I'm attempting to convey. I don't have all of the answers, obviously, but I do know that we can hustle backwards when it comes to relationships when we do anything that counteracts the growth or attraction of a suitable person or relationship.

Spiritual Life.

Spiritually hustling backwards. This hits home with me big time. I believe in a creator, I believe in God, I know what his word says. I know what he would like to see me do and how he'd like to see in me as a man. But I hustle backwards in this area. I tell him I love him. I tell him I want to follow his word. I tell him I know that he controls everything in my life. I know that all the good that happens in my life comes from him. But yet, I don't always act like I'm a follower of Jesus Christ. Maybe you've been there too. Am I "on your street?"

Kanye West has a song called "Devil in a new dress" and the chorus says: *"We love Jesus but you done learned a lot from Satan."* You have to be careful when hustling backwards in spirituality. As for me, not sharing my testimony with others is hustling backwards. You cannot expect a blessing when you're not blessing anyone else...in some way. If you want joy, success, love, healing, peace, money, fulfillment, growth in all areas of your life, good health, strong relationships, etc., you should wish for or pray for others to have those same things as well. It's hustling backwards if you don't.

Family.

You want to have a successful, beautiful family. You want to provide for that family. You want all the trappings of success for your family. Things like a nice house, a nice car, nice clothing, good and clean food, and family vacations. Just to name a few. You proclaim what you want. You work hard for it. Yet, you are so dedicated to your career and hobby that you hardly see your family let alone spend time with them. As a matter of fact, most of the time you get home so late that the kids are already asleep. Sometime you leave the house so early that they are still asleep when you leave. They never see you. I get it though, you're hustling right? No, that hustling backwards.

Be mindful of the many things we can do to take away from our family while at the same time providing for our families. Hustling backwards in this area can be the most costliest areas that we can do this in. Losing money and health is one thing. As important as they are, they don't compare at all to losing your family. The comparison isn't even close!

Business owners/Management.

Business owners hustle backwards too. They want to have a great staff working for them but the training is sub par. They don't invest in it. At times, speaking down to the team and never genuinely uplifting them. They don't show their team the respect they deserve on a consistent basis but expect the business to grow and flourish. That's hustling backwards. You worked so hard to get the business started but cutting corners when it comes to your product to save a dime here and there doesn't make sense. You may be saving money but the quality of your product is dropping. That's hustling backwards. Invest in your business, your team, your product, and most importantly, in yourself.

To conclude, hustling backwards is simply the mindset and activity of self-sabotage. You can knowingly and unknowingly do this. You can intentionally be doing this and not even know it. Seek out mentorship in business and management.

Please know that hustling backwards is something that we all do at times. It's not a death sentence to your evolvement and growth but it can surely be a detriment. There are levels to hustling backwards. I'll expound on that some other time. The important thing is for you to recognize it and modify your behavior to avoid the pitfalls of Hustling Backwards.

BLIND SPOTS

After weeks of rest, rehabilitation, and therapy, I was finally able to make an appointment with Dr. Penelope Suter. She came highly recommended and known to be very busy. She's an Optometrist that specializes in optometry and vision therapy. She has extensive experience with people who have had a brain injury. I was eager to see her. I heard good things about her. I really wanted to see what was the issue with my right eye.

Following an initial extensive examination that lasted an hour and included numerous peripheral vision tests, she concluded that I had a blind spot in my right eye. A profound blind spot. She was able to pinpoint it. During the examinations I noticed it too. My overall vision was good but surely the blind spot existed. The development of this blind spot was actually my first sign of stroke.

Obviously, I wasn't aware of that because if I had been, I would've went to the hospital immediately. When I was in the mall walking with Cicely, I had what's called a TIA, a Transient Ischemic Attack. This is known as a mini stroke or a warning stroke. It's called a warning stroke because in many cases it precedes a bigger attack in the near future. This was surely the case for me. Today, this blind spot has resulted in me having to scan to the right often and reading backwards to compensate. At times, I can't read in my normal reading pattern. When I drive I have to have my head on a swivel more in order to avoid breaking the law or running into someone.

Let me elaborate a little on the story I told you earlier. When I was at dinner with Cicely, I called myself being a gentleman. I offered her my last piece of sweet & sour chicken. I remember telling her how delightful the food was, especially the chicken, and then saying, *"You can have my last piece of chicken if you like."* She replied with a laugh, *"That's not your last piece. You have a piece right there!"* I looked down at my plate. I said, *"Where?"* She pointed. *"There!"* she said. To my surprise, there was another piece of chicken on my plate...to the right to be exact. The piece of chicken was in my blind spot. All I had to do was slightly move my head to the right and I would've seen my last piece of chicken. I could've saved face. By the way, I ate that last piece of chicken.

One sign of a stroke is sudden vision issues, arm weakness, and slurred speech amongst other things. Dr. Suter prescribed some eyewear for me and suggested aggressive therapy so that I could learn to manage my life with the blind spot. This included exercises on the computer and home exercises for my vision.

This entire situation was teaching me valuable lessons. One of them I was very familiar with but I wouldn't act on it. In my life, there have been great opportunities and blessings directly in front of me but I haven't seen them because of blind spots. I believe that we all deal with blind spots at some point in our lives. Some of the biggest blessings that you'll have assigned to your life are right in front of you...slightly to the right. That extra burst of energy that you need to go that extra mile to achieve excellence is on your right, but you don't see it because of the blind spot. The ingenuity to create and bring to life an idea is slightly to your right. I suggest you scan more often. There is more favor for you but you don't notice because of the blind spot. There are opportunities for you to serve and be a blessing others but it's in your blind spot. The great opportunity that you wish for, it's right there in your blind spot! Scan more.

I've always had a heart for serving people. I've always had the talent to speak in front of various audiences. I've always had the desire to stand in front of people to share but I didn't wholeheartedly pursue it until I had a stroke. I knew of this opportunity but it was in my blind spot. I saw this as something I'd do in a few years. But unbeknownst to me, God wanted me to purse this vision sooner than later.

Let's talk more in depth about blind spots and the reason you don't see your greatness and miracles within you.

1. **Distractions.** We are too engulfed in other people. We choose to live a lifestyle of being casual when it comes to what we allow in our lives. We need to modify our process of choosing our friends, acquaintances, business partners/ ventures, and significant others/ spouses.

2. **Pride/Closed mind.** I don't recall the originator of this quote but I'll paraphrase, "He who claims to know it all, knows nothing." In the movie Pulp Fiction, the actor Ving Rhames played a menacing character named Marsellus Wallace. One of the most popular quotes he states in the movie, pertains to pride. He said, "Pride only hurts, it never helps." This is so true. Not being open to new ideas or ways of doing thing can create a blind spot in our lives. As smart and accomplished as we may feel we are, we don't know everything! We can always learn. We should seek opportunities to learn and get better in life.

3. **Prejudgment.** Some of our biggest blessings don't always come wrapped in the package that we think it should. Therefore, don't prejudge people, jobs, seminars, churches, business opportunities, etc. You never know what's awaiting you. You never know what God has planned for you. Several years ago I was approached with a "business opportunity". I was very skeptical. I decided not to

prejudge the information and give it a good listen. The decision not to prejudge has positively impacted every area of my life.

4. **Seek coaching.** Sometime other people can see things about us or in us that we can't see ourselves. Being able to take coaching or constructive criticism from a trusted colleague or friend can be supremely beneficial. Allow people to help you uncover your blind spot.

5. **Not thinking big enough.** We can simply have goals and dreams that are too small. When we do, we don't think we can achieve certain levels in life therefore we don't seek higher goals. We can get blinded by our short sighted vision. We should think outside the box and believe that we can go further in life than our circumstances dictate. Stop limiting your capacity and ability to achieve.

Having a blind spot in one area of your life can affect other areas as well. The blind spot in my right eye caused me to temporarily have my license suspended. This meant I couldn't drive a car myself. I had to be driven by someone else. When I did finally start driving I had to drive differently as I stated prior. I had to pay closer attention and take more time making certain maneuvers. The blind spot affects the way that I read sometime. When I'm getting dressed I have to pay closer attention. I can't tell you how many times I put my t-shirt on backwards or missed a button on my dress shirt. All because of the blind spot.

You can't be closed minded in one area of your life and it not affect another area. If you are prideful in one area of your life, you are likely that way in all areas of your life. A know-it-all in his/her home life is likely the same at work and could negatively affect their career. If a person doesn't see themselves achieving high goals at work and getting promoted in the future, there is a good chance that they also don't dream and have big goals for their family as well. Get my point? Don't departmentalize blind spots. If you decide to work on your blind spots in one area of your life, know that you are also improving other areas as well. Dedicate yourself to removing blind spots in your life.

DO IT FOR THE DOUBTERS

I am so inspired by doubters. I'm so inspired by haters. I'm so inspired by failure and setbacks. I don't know where this part of me came from but I've always been that way. First of all, I've always been a person who has wanted to look like a success, present myself as if nothing is wrong or ever has been. I carry myself with a certain swag. I can remember being this way at a very young age. I didn't grow up with advantages that would position me to have the nicer things like Nike shoes and name brand clothes. I grew up in what's known as "The Projects" of East Bakersfield, CA which was very drug and gang infested in the mid-1980s. Internally, I had all of those things. Internally I felt it was my birthright to be successful. Now, when I do read about the traits of a Capricorn (born in mid January) I have learned it's in our

DNA to feel that way. We don't like to look bad. We don't like to be embarrassed. We like to always come off like we have it all together. Of course, we don't always have it all together but some of us have a way of managing our disappointment or should I say, disciplining our disappointment. I've had that trait since I could remember. Discipline my disappointment. I'm inspired by the doubters. I'll be honest, I do what I do partially because some people either don't think that I can do it or they don't want to see me do it. I'll admit, I have never actually heard someone tell me that they don't want to see me succeed or that they have these negative wishes for me to fail. As much as I hear people say how many haters they have, I wonder how many of those people really have actually heard that from the mouth of someone. I'm sure there are some people who have actually heard that from someone but in most cases, probably not. Usually it's something that is assumed based on the energy that the so-called hater exudes. It's the energy that they give off when you are in the same proximity. You both may be at a business function or at the mall. When you cross paths with one another, there is a certain agitating energy that they give you. This energy lets you know that they can care less about you and they are totally indifferent to your success or failure in life. As a matter of fact, they likely lean more towards your failure. What I've learned is that people don't necessarily always want to see you fail or not perform up to expectation because they dislike you. I've found that most people that doubt you are people who are just tired of seeing you win.

For example, social media. There are some beautiful people on my newsfeed, and I applaud them all and I hope they applaud me as well. Nonetheless, I have to say this. Some people do the same selfie everyday. Sometimes multiple times a day! The same position. The same smile. Basically, the same everything... everyday! Now look, I'm a selfie taker myself, I don't shy away from them; however, there's a limit for me. Most of the time people aren't actually saying anything at all. Now, let me say this, I like these people. Some of them I actually love. I'm just being honest here. After awhile I just get tired of seeing them. Especially if it's a constant daily ritual repeated over and over again. Here's my point. I feel that's the same thing that happens with the doubters. They're just tired of seeing you win! They're just tired of seeing you shine! I'm sure most of them are thinking, "Yes he looks happy and he's making things happen in his life. He's successful but I'm sure he has problems. There is something wrong in this picture." I'll be the first to admit, I am not perfect. I don't know all of the answers. I don't always do or say the right things. I have some shortcomings in my life but I humbly say that these problems in my life are far between. I don't stew in mess. My life isn't circled by the vultures of negativity. But as anyone is accustomed to in this life, there are going to be some problems to overcome. There are going to be some walls that you are going to hit. You will have a few "strokes". People don't want to see you win. The doubters surely are tired of seeing you win. Trust me, it's usually a reflection of what's going on in their lives. Most of the time it's because of their own limited belief system. Therefore when they see you living beyond what they feel that they can do, they doubt you. And for some crazy reason, I'm inspired by this. I love it.

You have big dreams. You have goals. You have deadlines to hit. You have projects to complete. You have a goal of a new home or getting a promotion at work. Maybe you have a desire to take your relationship with someone to the next level. I want you to do it! I want you to do it for your family and for yourself. But I also want you to include the doubters. Do it for the doubters! The doubters need love too. The doubters need inspiration too. Let them fuel you. Understand that they have been put in your life for a reason. That reason is to help you get to the next level in life. They are like ladders. You can use them to climb to higher heights. Learn to view your doubters just like that. Love your doubters. Cherish your doubters because you need them.

I can remember being in the hospital after having the strokes. The people I thought about first were the people that I love and that I know love me as well. I thought about my children and my close dear friends. I thought about some of my coworkers, my church family, my basketball officiating fraternity, and my business partners. I also thought about my doubters. I thought about some of the people I knew for a fact, didn't mind seeing me in the position that I was in. They were indifferent in every sense of the word. As a matter of fact, some of them felt that I deserved to be in the position I was in because of some things that they felt I did wrong in the past. Some things that I've said in the past. The way I've carried myself in the past. The way I've won in the past. The way I've always taken on losses in the past. Always coming back with a vengeance. Always finding my way back to the top. Finding myself in favor. I feel that God has shined on my whole life. I'm sure many of you rightfully feel the exact same way. I'm grateful for it. God has shown me unmerited grace. He's given me that gift. He's surely given that gift to many people but my relationship with God is intimate and personal. I'm sure the same for you.

I hate the fact that sometimes I dim my shine. Mistakenly, I dim my light at times because I don't want to offend someone. But I have many moments when I walk with my shoulders back, and my chest out, my head high, allowing my light to shine. I do that while thinking about the doubters at times. This is how you master setbacks. This is how you engulf yourself in personal development and use it to your advantage. The more you take in personal development, the more you work on you, the more you read the positive books and listen to the positive messages, it perspires through your skin. It pours out so much that it makes it very easy for you to be thankful for your doubters. You'll pray and love your doubters. Like I said earlier, your doubters deserve to be happy too. There's nothing wrong with having negative forces against you in life. The late great Jim Rohn said, "You can't fly without gravity." Think about it. If there was no gravity you'd just be floating around as a wandering generality. You can fly because of the negative forces. These forces actually help you fly to higher heights.

Here are five reasons you should bounce back, win, and shine for your doubters. I'll also give you five ways to use this energy:

1. **Gives you clarity on your goal.** Doubters sharpen your work ethic. They sharpen your focus. I can recall when I was in rehabilitation for the strokes, I'd sometime think about my doubters as I worked on walking again. It gave me clarity on what I had to do that day in therapy. It fueled my drive.

2. **It allows your competitive juices to flow with more fervor.** You may not always be in a competitive environment (sports, business rivalry) but nonetheless you are a very competitive person,. When you think about your doubters and your goals, it makes you want to compete like never before. Here's the kicker though. You don't necessarily want to compete against them yet you want to compete against their expectations of you. It keeps you young, vibrant, and with that certain "bounce".

3. **The doubters need inspiration.** I've been in situations where I knew someone didn't have the best hope for me. They didn't like to see me win for whatever reason. Yet as time went on, I've noticed a change of heart and energy

towards me. I believe that change happened because of how I came back from my situation. I've received some form of communication from a few of these people expressing their delight and inspiration based on what they've witnessed. Keep in mind, a doubter doesn't have to be your enemy. In many cases, they actually become your friend. They say, "The sweetest revenge is massive success." I say, "The sweetest revenge is your haters becoming your lover, your doubters becoming believers in you."

4. **People are watching you.** They need to see your example. Family, friends, and acquaintances need to see you come back and show resilience. They need to see you brush off your shoulders when you fall. Why? So that when they fall they know that they too can bounce back and use their experience to inspire others.

5. **They are indicators of your future success.** If you have lots of doubters be happy. If you just have a few doubters but they talk a lot, be happy! This simply means that if you use the experience the right way, you have a big future ahead.

Here are five ways to use the energy fueled by your doubters:

1. **Let it fuel your creativity, ingenuity, and your work ethic.** This book that you are reading now was partially inspired and energized by my doubters.

2. **Walk like a peacock!** Be proud. Regardless of your failure, setback, or amount of doubters you have, walk tall with confidence. You are not your mistakes or setbacks.

3. **Serve others more. Give to other people.** Use that fire of your doubters to serve the world. Don't get distracted by your detractors. This can be achieved by focusing on serving someone else. Give at your church, give clothing to Goodwill, visit someone in the hospital and help someone finance a business.

4. **Insanely pursue your "far out audacious" goals.**

5. **Become a noticeably new you.** Work on you, more. Go to the gym, more. Eat better, more. Take care of your health with more intensity. Be more on point with your finances. Be better in your relationship. Be more consistent in your spirituality. Engulf yourself in personal development by reading a book and listening to positive messaging. Let it become all about you becoming better.

These are all the things that I used in my personal situation and dealing with the doubters. I'm quite sure that they can be beneficial to you as well as you navigate through your doubters. Remember, do it for them too!

Bonus eBook:

R.E.S.E.T

HIT THE RESET BUTTON IN YOUR LIFE

Terrance Minnoy

ABOUT THE AUTHOR

Through all the struggles and the odds against you, still success has manifested in all areas of your life. You've read the self development books, you've attended seminars, you've encouraged others, given to causes, and your star is rising in the business world or corporate America. Your foundation of faith and belief in God is as solid as ever.

What happens when that faith and internal fortitude is put to the ultimate test? Are you that same person? Is your steel will remaining unbreakable?

My story of recovery following three strokes in 24 hours and the ascent of my purpose driven message through this blessing, will surely inspire and encourage you. We each have a "reservoir of resilience" within us. The key is the proper maintenance of that reservoir in order for us to swiftly tap into it when life-changing moments happen.

My free E-book, 5 Steps to Resilience in Adverse Moments, showcases exactly what I did to not only fully recover, but to R.E.S.E.T and get to a new level.

To RESET, it can be magical, delightful, rewarding, and even spiritual if you have the right perspective. If you do it right you can change outcomes in your business, relationships, career, and the trajectory of your entire life.

Sure, there may be some pain and discomfort to endure in the process but you'll be better for it. As a matter of fact, regardless of the reason you have to reset, if you don't grow or come out better for it as a person, I would argue that the reset was pointless.

Sure your relationships may have improved, you may have overcome an illness, your business may have grown or you recaptured that large account, but the key to a reset is that you become better through the process.

I consider myself a "RESET expert". As the saying goes, I've been great at "turning lemons into lemonade."

Here's my story.

At the age of 44, a blood clot lodged in my brain stem, broke into pieces and caused me to have three strokes in 24 hours. The cause of the blood clot is still unknown today. The doctors explained that it was a miracle that I survived considering the size and location of the blood clots. The left side of my body was paralyzed. The brain damage affected my speech, vision, and my motor skills. I spent a few weeks in the hospital followed by months of intense rehabilitation.

After lots of prayer, hard work, and dedication, I miraculously made it back to my career and living my life without limitations. I am as close to 100% as a person could be after the health crisis I experienced. My focus now is living my life on purpose each and every day. Not only am I physically thriving, am I living my passion by writing and speaking to others about defying the odds and overcoming adversity. My friend, Stephen Elcano, says that I'm a "Dealer of Hope". As you can imagine, I had to do a major RESET. I hit the reset button with both hands!

RESET is defined as, "to set again". The definition also mentions words like, establish, arrange, and position. It's the science and art of reestablishing, rearranging, repositioning oneself to attain a positive outcome.

Most people think of reset as it pertains to our natural reaction following a setback or some type of adversity. RESETs are also necessary following the victories in our lives. In life we are always calibrating and adjusting somewhat but during our journey we will have "interruptions" that cause us to RESET in a more intentional and organized way. Keep in mind these interruptions can be positive as well as negative. I've come up with an acronym for the word R.E.S.E.T. Each letter has a specific meaning that I see as steps that can be taken during the reset process, regardless of the reason you may need to reset. I used each step during my recovery.

- **Rest**
- **Evaluate**
- **Strategize**
- **Expectancy**
- **Take Action**

RESET!

R – REST

I used each of these steps during my stroke recovery. I can confidently say they worked and they will work for you too. Before I go into what each letter means, I ask that you stop here and Reflect. Take two minutes and think about some moments in your life that caused you to reset:

- Was it health related? Unexpected illness, healing
- Job/Career related? Job loss, promotion, relocation
- Family changes/crisis? Financial, loss of a loved one, birth of a child
- Environmental? New associations, loss of a relationship or new relationship, election outcome
- Spiritual? Baptism, better understanding of beliefs or change of religion

Notice that I didn't just assume negative happenings?

A reset can also take place even when we look to take the next step up in our lives. When I suffered the strokes back in early 2015, I spent the first 8 days of my recovery at San Joaquin Community Hospital in Bakersfield, Ca. One thing I didn't do was use my energy to constantly ask God, "Why?" I spent that time getting some rest. I laid still. It's not a secret that we do much of our development as people when we are in solitude or asleep. As we rest, our muscles rebuild and recover, illnesses subside, and comfort settles in following pain. We pay more attention to that inner voice when we are laying still and quiet. The inner voice can be a voice of reason, encouragement, hope, prosperity, or recovery.

REST is essential to the reset process. You have to gather yourself and be still for a moment before taking your next step. Depending on what you're dealing with and how you process things, the length of the rest period varies from person to person. You may need a month following the loss of a loved one, a few weeks after a relationship breakup, a couple weeks following a knee surgery, or a few days after losing a large account.

Everyone is wired differently and requires different things. I've literally reset by simply sitting in my car quietly for 20 minutes during a rough start to the day. Rest is a must if you want to bounce back and come back stronger and smarter.

A rest period is also essential following the victories in your life. Maybe you got a promotion at work, closed a big account, got a good health report, received a financial blessing, or bounced back from a health crisis. A few years ago, I was unexpectedly approached about an opportunity within our company. The interview and offer process took about three weeks. I prepared day and night for the interview. Over the years I had positioned myself for great things to happen to me and to my excitement the time had come, I was offered the job! Unknowingly, it came with a substantial pay increase. I was elated! Excited and emotionally drained, I took off work the following day. I celebrated a little with some friends but I took most of the time to be still, reflect, and start thinking about my new chapter. That day of rest and leisure served me well. Since I was still in my old role at that time I refreshed and prepared to finish strong. You don't have to always be in pursuit of the next accomplishment following a victory.

Stop and "smell the roses" to reset.

Ask yourself these questions:
- Am I sleeping enough?
- Do I take time to be still when I'm disappointed?
- Do I take a moment to quietly reflect following a victory?

E – EVALUATE

Following a setback of any kind you have to take a moment to evaluate the situation before you come up with a recovery plan. **Ask yourself these questions:**

• What happened? Was this self-inflicted or out of your hands?
• What does this mean moving forward?
• Am I in denial about what has happened?
• Can I grow from this situation?
• Who can help me in this situation?

I didn't fight the fact that I was a stroke survivor after realizing what happened. I came to understand that it wasn't my fault and there was nothing I could've done to prevent it. I lived a pretty healthy lifestyle prior to the strokes. I ate fairly well, I didn't smoke, I worked out regularly, and I didn't have high cholesterol or high blood pressure.

During the recovery process I recall constantly saying to myself, *"I'm coming back from this."* I wasn't sure that it would happen at the time but I believed it could. I was in bad shape. Looking into the mirror and being honest with yourself is important in the reset process. If you immediately attempt to fix the matter, you won't learn from the situation and how to avoid it in the future (if possible).

S – STRATEGIZE

Here is when the magic starts to happen! This step is where you begin to utilize all of your internal and external tools to begin planning your comeback. You can't reset unless you have a strategy to do so. It doesn't just happen. It has to be intentional. If your "bounce back" or recovery is really important to you then this step must be done with intention. It must be well thought out.

I was taken to HealthSouth Rehabilitation Center after being hospitalized for 8 days and this is when the strategy for my recovery began. A good friend of mine, Jerry, has worked as a therapist at HealthSouth for years so I knew about their great reputation. Over the years I'd also heard about their success rates and that they put their patients through an intense program. The program required hard work and I would have to fully participate in my rescue. With that in mind, my strategy was put in motion. I was going to be intentional about my RESET. I was so intentional and ready for the challenge that I had my favorite pair of gym shoes brought to the hospital. They were an Army colored pair of camouflage Nike cross trainers. I was ready for the "battle to recover".

Here was my plan:
- Work hard
- Rest
- Move my left side
- Learn to walk again
- Walk out of the hospital

I was so steadfast and intentional about this strategy that I spoke it, wrote it visualized it, and prayed on it. I even had people take pictures and videos of me during the process because I wanted my story documented from the beginning to FULL recovery!

E – EXPECTANCY

This is THE most important step in the RESET process!

Expectancy makes it all work. It's the gas to the engine. Without it the car goes nowhere. Without high expectancy your plan to reset is futile. It doesn't matter what situation you find yourself in, it doesn't matter what industry you work in, or the type of project you're working on, without high expectancy your strategy is destined to fail in most cases. While lying in the hospital bed I always expected something to improve. In fact I expected progress every day. As I mentioned earlier my left side was affected by the strokes and I couldn't move my left extremities at all.

I was always hopeful things would improve but I won't lie, I worried a little that it would never happen. Despite my temporary worry, I would imagine my fingers, toes, and ankle functioning normally. I would pray, I would stare at them and I would try my absolute best to move them but I couldn't. In my mind I could clearly see them moving but in reality I couldn't do it. No matter what I remained hopeful. I had high expectations that it would happen and after eleven days, it happened!

I didn't sleep very well in the hospital; I was awake at all times of the night and morning. One morning at 3:30am I was overwhelmed with joy when I was able move one of my toes on my left foot! I moved it about one centimeter. Yes, that was it but I was so excited! With disregard to the time of night, I sent out a group text message to about twelve friends that simply read, *"I moved my toe on my left foot!"* From that point on my expectancy was heightened. During your reset process the smallest of victories can be so encouraging and give you lots of momentum.

Don't discount the power of progress...even the slightest. Celebrate and praise your progress. To me, the greatest example of high expectancy is found in the Bible. It's the story of David and Goliath. Here's the scene for those who may not know the story. David was a small Israeli shepherd boy. Goliath was a Philistine giant. He was at least nine feet tall and terrifying. He constantly called out the Israeli army to a death battle. No one in the army would step up to fight him. They were all afraid. Goliath was heavily armored and extremely confident.

Finally, David volunteered to fight Goliath. Goliath thought it was a joke and professed that he was going to kill David. Guess what? David was confident too. Furthermore, he had high expectancy. It was so high that he boldly announced to Goliath that he was going to cut his head off and feed his carcass to the birds and wild animals. He quickly approached Goliath and killed him by slinging large rocks at his head. David evaluated the situation. He strategized. Then he showed high expectancy by quickly approaching Goliath and taking action. He later became the king of Israel.

This is how I demonstrated high expectancy: I wrote it, visualized it, and prayed on it. I even had people take pictures and videos of me during the process because I wanted my story documented from the beginning to FULL recovery!

This is how I demonstrated high expectancy:
• Constantly spoke about making a comeback. *When vs. If*
• Immediately purchased an in home weight set to workout
• Posted encouraging signs throughout my home
• Spent time with my support team i.e. friends, church, mentors
• Eagerly participated in rehab

Here are a few tips to help encourage expectancy in you:
• Seek testimonials of others
• Have a "Can do" attitude
• Face challenges with confidence
• Help someone else overcome a challenge
• Develop a support team

T – TAKE ACTION

Nothing I've said matters at all if action isn't taken! It's that simple. Wait, actually it's not simple at all. I've learned that what's easy to do is also easy not to do. Make a decision. Decide that you are going to reset and that you'll be better than before. Taking action has been the driving force of my recovery. It's been two years now and I'm still work hard to be better than I was prior to the strokes. I want to be better physically, mentally, and spiritually. I want to be better in my career, in business, and in my relationships with others. Like strategizing, taking action must be done intentionally. Be bold and intentional when you decide to take action. I took "all out massive action" in my journey to reset. As I stated, I purchased weights for my home, I was faithful to my rehab therapy and I consistently went to the gym to strengthen my body. I modified my diet and made sure I took my medicines as prescribed by my physicians. I constantly worked on improving me. I'd like to mention that the byproduct of going through this process to RESET is a lesson in personal and professional development. You will become better! You will be a better friend, a better parent, a better business person, a better leader, and much more. This is why this process must be intentional and not taken lightly. Your family and your future are depending on it.

Lastly, become proficient at these steps to RESET so that you can pass the experience on to someone else. Help someone else reset and overcome an adverse situation or help someone reset to get to the next level of success in their lives. Allow your RESET to serve others. Sharing my story has surely been my mission and helping others has been my reward.

R.E.S.E.T

Bonus eBook:

5 STEPS
TO RESILIENCE IN
ADVERSE MOMENTS

Terrance Minnoy

A few days ago I took my 8 year old daughter to a popular park in town. This particular park is known for its upgraded scenery which includes ducks and geese that live in the ponds. We tried to get the duck's attention to have them come to us so we can feed them but for the most part, they stayed their distance. They'd rather you throw the bread out to them, and when they do, they'd glide so smoothly across the water. It looked like they didn't have a care in the world. They looked peaceful, graceful, and beautiful. My daughter commented, *"They swim so easily."* The comment made me think about what's really going on as they swim. I know for a fact that they look calm and graceful on top of the water but underneath the water they are feverishly paddling their feet. There is lots of commotion going on underneath the surface. Nevertheless, their "response" to the commotion is pure flawlessness.

I feel that's the story of my life. I seem to have it all together, polished, and able to conquer the world. But underneath my surface has been commotion and adversity. Don't get me wrong, I'm thankful for it. I really am. If it hadn't been for all of it, I wouldn't be who I am today. I've learned that it's all about how we respond to adverse situations that matter.

Hello, I'm Terrance Minnoy. I was raised on the eastside of Bakersfield, CA in the '80s. I was raised by a single mother, Dorothy Coleman, in a drug and gang infested neighborhood. I was never involved with drugs and gangs but I did fall into some of the other perils of low income housing neighborhoods like; fighting, stealing, cheating, and promiscuity at a young age. Lucky for me, I was always an outstanding athlete and that serve me when it came to the neighborhood "brass" protecting me from their wiles and it gave me hope that I could make something of myself.

In high school I became a basketball star, student body president, homecoming king and I received a basketball scholarship to a Division I school. I left the state to follow my dreams of earning a college degree and possibly playing professional basketball.

Leaving home was not easy and I left with a heavy heart. You see, at the age of 17 I became a teenage father. For those of you who have been in similar situations or know someone who has, you understand the relationship drama and heartache the situation can bring. I wouldn't wish that on anyone.

By the grace of God I went on to receive my masters degree in business, became a sales leader in multiple industries; retail, the beverage industry, and part-time network marketing. I continued on to a successful pharmaceutical sales career earning the coveted "six-figure salary", I had it all; home ownership, luxury cars, bank accounts, financial investments, I usher at church and I give to charities, etc. I'm in a good place, wouldn't you agree? I truly have no complaints. As a matter of fact, I've done all that I can over the years to continue to become a better person. I've read books, attended seminars, listened to positive messaging in my car, and tried to be a blessing to others when I could. I'd say that I was filled to the brim with positivity and optimism. Some would say I overflowed. Considering where I'd come from and all that I had gone through to get to this point, I'm in a good place.

In early 2015, without warning, I had a stroke! Not one stroke. Not two strokes. But three strokes in twenty-four hours. I was paralyzed on the left side of my body for two weeks, I lost my peripheral vision in my right eye, my speech was slurred, and the brain damage had me "seeing things" flying around my room and out of people's mouth. I was in hospitals for almost a month. I had to learn to balance and walk again. I did aggressive therapy daily; including vision, occupational, cognitive, and physical therapy for about three months. To this day the definite causes of the strokes have not been found. I don't have a history of high blood pressure or high cholesterol. I have never smoked or done drugs. I eat fairly well. I have always worked out multiple times per week and my lifestyle isn't blatantly stressful.

THE STORY BEGINS

Adversity and pain is the alarm clock of life. Wake up Terrance! The universe has a way of doing that to each and everyone one of us. It doesn't matter who you are, the alarm will sound at some point in our lives. We can "snooze" it for a little while, sometimes a long while. Eventually, it's going to go off. Wake up!

Game on! Now what do you do? You may be strong and resilient when life is "good" but how do you respond when life rings the alarm. It happens to us all. It happens to every athlete, corporate executive, TV personality, worshiper, parent, accountant, bus driver, manager, pastor, architect, insurance broker, gold medalist, champion, and many many more. You get my point? The alarm will sound in your life.

My goal is to showcase, develop, and maintain that "reservoir" of resilience and strength within us. I want to help you graciously receive adversity in your life and use it to your advantage in the pursuit of success and happiness in all areas of life.

I'm thankful I was introduced to personal development some fifteen years ago. The teachings and tactics in my pursuit of personal development were vital in my efforts to overcome adverse moment in my life. I'd say that personal development is the main reason I stand strong as the man that I have become and achieved the levels of success that I have to this point. I believe that the principles that I fell back on to help me graciously receive and overcome the adversities a stroke(s) can bring to an individual, are the same principles that can drive a person to the ultimate success they are seeking.

I'd like to share, "5 Steps to Resilience in Adverse Moments." It's important that you embrace and practice these concepts even BEFORE an adverse situation comes your way (the alarm WILL sound) so when these principles are needed they are automatically pulled from within your inner being, that reservoir.

Let me tell you, even as I lay motionless on my bedroom floor following one of the strokes, I didn't "abandon ship". My reservoir of resilience was activated immediately! Allow me to share how you can ensure your reservoir is properly maintained and ready to serve you when you need it most, at the sound of the alarm.

ACCEPTANCE/RELEASE

When one goes through an adverse event in their lives, especially if it's sudden, you need all of your healing energy 100% focused on just that...healing. When your mental energy is focused on, *"why did this happen to me," "this isn't fair," "this isn't so, I live a healthy lifestyle," "no way this is happening I'm a faithful spouse,"* etc. then the healing process is actually delayed. You want that energy to be your friend immediately. When I found myself on my bedroom floor, after a minute or so I realized I was having a stroke, *"out of nowhere!"* is what I thought to myself. Once this sunk into my brain after 5 minutes of being on the floor and unable to move, I accepted the fact... I was having a stroke. I didn't go into, "why/how mode," I accepted the realization. When I did so, as afraid as I was at the time, it gave me power. I didn't use my energy to wrestle but I was able to use my energy to start the thought process continuum that would lead me through this valley in my life.

I believe that there is a reason that attendees at an Alcoholics Anonymous meeting introduce themselves by saying, *"Hi I'm XYZ...and I'm an alcoholic."* They have accepted that fact. That's the starting point to recovery. Now they can access and activate the energy needed to travel the rough journey to recovery. They no longer waste energy fighting the disease. They don't accept their fate (inevitable fate if they continue to lose the battle), they accept the circumstances. There is power in accepting current circumstances because they can always be changed.

This was a time of **R.E.S.E.T** for me. I accepted the fact that I had a "new normal" now. I won't get into it much here but hitting the reset button is vital at this point. Rest, Evaluate, Strategize, Expectancy, and Take Action.

I can remember being in the ambulance on that surprisingly quiet ride across town to the hospital, needles in my arms, and vomit on my shirt...I'm Terrance, and I'm a stroke victim!

VISUALIZATION

I've learned over the years that the brain is able to learn more, and more efficiently, with pictures and not just words. I found this to be true in many situations in my life. The more I visualize the ball going through the hoop the chances of that happening for me tended to happen more often. The more I visualized being recognized in front of my peers, it tended to happen. The more I visualized the house I lived in, the car I'd drive, the amount of money in the bank account, things tended to move in that direction. Therefore, when I had the strokes, I visualized just as I did before...but even more.

On the second day I was in the hospital, after being told I had three strokes and that I'm lucky I'm not quadriplegic and blind, I began taking pictures of myself in the hospital bed. I did the same thing when I went to the rehabilitation hospital, I took pictures and video. I even allowed more visitors to see me (at my family and hospitals displeasure) because I was in constant "movie mode", visualizing myself as the star in my triumphant story.

What did I visualize?

I constantly and vividly pictured myself running down the court as a basketball official. Driving on the highway to work, working out in the gym, on my post as an usher at church, playing ball with my daughter, speaking in the front of a room with thousands attending, writing a book, sharing my story with others, and much, much more.

DEPOSIT INTO OTHERS (DO SOME PUSH-UPS!)

The #1 thing that I learned after the strokes and it continues to be a confirmation to this day, "There is power in serving others!" We work so hard to gain power in this life and it's an awesome feeling when you lend that power to someone else. Giving yourself away to others is only giving to you two-fold.

While listening to a radio preacher years ago I heard him say something that strongly stuck in my memory. He mentioned that whatever you find yourself praying for or in need of, make that same request for someone else. He said that's how you receive what you want. The "universe" works that way. Ok. So what did that look like in my particular moment of adversity? I started doing "push-ups"…pushing someone else up either through genuine edification, compliments, or simply a smiling pleasantry (even though my smile was crooked). I'd continued to text friends encouraging words from the hospital bed. I even forgave some debts owed to me. I just wanted to make others feel good, happy, and encouraged. See, this is what I needed as well. I diligently prayed for others in the hospital battling the effects of stroke. I made sure my charitable giving continued while in the hospital and not working.

Push others up. Push others up.

I was laser focused on this. Now is the time to be the ultimate selfless man. Keep in mind; I also did my best to live this way even BEFORE the strokes. That's the key, do it now before your adverse event. Proactively fill your resilience reservoir. We are born with a natural resilience reservoir within us. The problem is that we only pay any attention to this stored up resilience when we have an adverse moment, reaching for a goal, taking on a new project or completing a task, like finishing a paper in two hours when you knew the due date two months ago. You got it done because you were able to tap into that reservoir. Proactively fill your resilience reservoir. One way to do this is by doing "push-ups". And you thought they were only good for building biceps and triceps. They can also build your resilience reserve.

The last point I'll make on this subject is a concept that I want you to embrace as I have. We all believe that giving back is a good thing. We give back to our communities, our parents, institutions we care about, etc. I want you to start looking at it this way. GIVE when you're on your BACK. When you're in an adverse moment or on your "back", if you can muster up the strength and energy to do so, give to someone else. You don't always have to give money either. Give your positive thoughts, kind words, deeds, or time. Give back when you're on your back.

CHECK THE NOISE ("SURROUND NOISE")

Watching a movie in our home theatre with surround sound is the best! We love it. It makes the entire movie experience better. Hearing the voices and music from all around us is comforting and enjoyable. The same is true when it comes to hearing certain voices for encouragement when you are going through adverse times. The sound of someone voice or just their mere presence can be healing in itself.

During tough times or while dealing with an adverse moment, be careful who you allow to be that voice in your ear or that shoulder you decide to lean on. During my recovery this was a priority for me. I even requested that certain people (that I love) not be allowed to visit me in the hospital because they had a natural predisposition of negativity. Even by simply looking at them I'd likely have negative thoughts. I listened to more positive music and listened to uplifting talks and sermons. I even had my son bring positive books from my home library. Not that I was going to read them all the time but I wanted positive vibes surrounding me. I went as far as posting encouraging quotes on the walls in my room. I wanted to make sure that my "surround sound" was in the best working condition to serve my immediate need of watching this "movie" in peace. Check your surround sound system. You don't want to miss any detail of this movie, especially the triumphant ending.

DON'T ABANDON SHIP

Many of you have heard much of my preceding steps before. You read about it. Maybe you heard it being said on stage before. Perhaps your parent or an uncle would say these things to you. Maybe you believe it all or just some of it. It's somewhere in your resilience reservoir. You tap into it occasionally. As a matter of fact, when someone you know was going through a tough and adverse moment, you encouraged them. You quoted something you heard at a seminar, through a Ted Talk, on the radio, or saw it played out on television. You liked it. You shared it. You believe wholeheartedly in it. BUT what happens when it's you in the hospital, going through the divorce, loss of a job, get a bad medical report, or suddenly find yourself in an adverse moment as I did. What do you do now? I am asking you to not abandon ship. As a ship captain is sworn to do, don't abandon ship. Go down with it if you have to. The same principle applies. Practice that which you believe and have been preaching to others during their time of need.

Take a look below at these quotes and/or sayings:
- "God wouldn't allow this unless He knew you were strong enough to handle it"
- "Play whatever hand you are dealt in life"
- "This setback is just a setup for a great comeback"
- "This will just make you stronger"
- "I'm praying for you. God got your back"
- "Stay positive"
- "Read something that's good for your soul. It helps"

Remember those? Remember all those quotes and sayings that you have fell in love with over your lifetime. Remember these "sayings" that resonate so much with you. Ok, lean on them yourself when you're going through your adverse moments! Don't turn your back now. These quotes, sayings, and all aspects of personal development serve you best…in adverse moments, when the chips are stacked against you, when the outcome looks bleak.

That's five ways to activate that resilience reservoir within you. I'll be sure to share more in the future. I hope this e-book is a blessing to you and those you share it with just as these concepts were a blessing to me when I was in a very tough place in my life. I look forward to hearing your stories of resilience in adverse moments and how these concepts helped you hit the "snooze" button of the alarm clock of life and awaken to the newfound burst of resilience from that reservoir within.

Now, it's time to take action. Make it happen, you can do it! You will make it to the mountain top with resilience. But remember, if you want to get to the top, you must first get off your bottom!!

Made in the USA
San Bernardino, CA
10 May 2018